Luther on Human Will

A thoughtful and precise abridgment
of the full text of
The Bondage of the Will by Martin Luther
based upon the 1823 translation from the Latin
by Henry Cole
as edited by
Leon C. Stansfield

with

***Ninety-Five Theses for the
21st Century Church***

by

Leon C. Stansfield, M.Ed., M.Div.

www.readthrutheword.com

Dedication

This book is dedicated to the greater spiritual health and maturity of the body of Jesus Christ — His church in the world, consisting of every believer in Jesus Christ — all those whom He has called, and who have believed to the saving of the soul.

Martin Luther by Hesse

Foreword

On the evening of October 31, 1517, Martin Luther nailed his famous *Ninety-Five Theses* to the Castle Church door in Wittenberg, Germany, sparking the Reformation. History was dramatically and significantly changed as the result of the life of Martin Luther. As we approach the five hundredth anniversary of that world-changing event perhaps history will be changed again — one life at a time — as the result of his writings.

Luther nails his Ninety-Five Theses to the Wittenberg Church door

As a young believer, I connected Martin Luther with the Biblical idea that "the just shall live by faith." I learned that I owed to Martin Luther and to Protestantism the restoration to the church of the concept that the basis for salvation is *by faith alone*, without works. But that is all I knew, and Martin Luther seemed to have lived so long ago.

In the course of time I obtained a copy of Martin Luther's greatest work *The Bondage of the Will*, as translated from the original Latin into English by J.I. Packer and O.R. Johnston. This book is Luther's considered, plainspoken and blunt reply to Desiderius Erasmus of Rotterdam who wrote, also in Latin, *The Diatribe*. In the *Diatribe* Erasmus discussed various aspects of Christian doctrine, and focused somewhat upon the important matter of the will of man. **His position was that man's will played an insignificant but decisive part in man's regeneration.** In *Bondage* Luther took Erasmus to task on this point, and showed how that Erasmus was, in essence, repeating the Pelagian heresy in a subtle, but extreme form.

Luther's **Bondage** pointed out a number of serious contradictions within Erasmus' **Diatribe**. It also made numerous major Biblical points regarding the roles which man's will, God's will, and God's grace have in the supernatural event of being born again by the Spirit of God. Having read this book several times, the author was impressed to read the book again and to mark *each assertion of Luther, each thesis statement*. He was surprised to count approximately *four hundred fifty such statements* after completing the task. This present book is designed to make accessible to a much wider audience the essence of Luther's great work:

1. present most of Luther's four-hundred fifty thesis statements
2. simplify Luther's theology as contained in **The Bondage of the Will**
3. omit extraneous discussion contained in **Bondage**
4. present **Ninety-Five Theses For The 21st Century Church**

This work is intended for the serious Christian reader, the Sunday school teacher, the Bible teacher, the pastor, the missionary, the minister of God. Just as in times past and present a great effort was (and is being) made by Martin Luther and a host of others to make the Holy Scriptures accessible to the average reader in his "heart language", so this work is an endeavor to make the great biblical truths restored to the church by Luther accessible to the average reader of the twenty-first century.

A key theological tenet re-birthed in the church during the Reformation — the distinction between **monergism** and **synergism** — has largely been lost over the past five centuries and the church as a whole has drifted far from this essential doctrinal truth. Having spent most of my life in churches which strongly hold to the synergistic position, I credit Martin Luther and God's Holy Spirit for opening up to me the truth which Luther so valiantly defends in his book. **Monergism**, as defined and explained by Martin Luther — although you will not see this word used in the entire text of his work — is the biblical doctrine that God, and God alone, is the source, the determiner, the power, and the author of a person's spiritual birth, while **synergism**, which is widely taught and preached in the evangelical churches, holds to the idea that, while God's grace is absolutely essential for salvation, and that a person's good works merit absolutely nothing toward salvation, in the final analysis it is the *individual person's choice* to become a Christian and to be born again, or to reject God's grace and be lost. Thus, in this belief man's will must work synergistically with God's will to bring about the new birth. Unavoidably, man's will is actually made superior to God's will. Eternal salvation becomes something which God offers to all mankind and which may be accepted or rejected. God is seen as One who never overrules a person's free will to choose. This view of God is perhaps the ultimate error of humanism, which is and has been the dominant worldview of our age. It is in reality an enormous distortion of the biblical doctrine of God, and the gospel of Jesus Christ.

The careful and serious student of the Bible will, by God's help, learn the distinction between these two doctrines and discover the great fallacy of the synergistic position. The careful biblical exegesis of Luther on this point needs to be known, discussed, taught, and used as a basis for all evangelism and Bible teaching in the church, Christian schools, home schools, Christian colleges, and seminaries. The implications for the tenets of faith held by all believers as discussed herein should influence all teaching and preaching of the gospel from the very youngest child to the eldest senior adult.

This present work will serve as the basis for gaining a clear understanding of Luther's biblical teaching on the topics of man's will, God's sovereign will, God's inscrutable will, the source of saving faith, and the grace of God in the salvation experience. The serious reader may confirm the many theses of this book, as well as the accuracy of this abridgement, by obtaining a complete copy of *The Bondage of the Will* in any edition and reading it for himself.

May God Himself bless the reader with a knowledge of His truth.
To God be all the glory!

Leon Stansfield   Stockton, CA   October 31, 2012

CONTENTS

Appendix

ILLUSTRATIONS

All illustrations, except as noted, including the cover picture, courtesy of the Archives of the Evangelical Lutheran Church in America.

Luther standing - 1817

Who Was Martin Luther?

Martin Luther was born in Eisleben, Thuringia, Germany, on November 10, 1483 to Hans and Margaret Luther. He was baptized the day after his birth on the feast of St. Martin of Tours, a sainted Roman soldier, from whom his name was taken. His parents were poor, his father being a laborer in the copper mines. They moved to Mansfield during Martin's first year. Later his father became a community leader, elected to the city council there. His father prospered and by 1511 was owner in a number of mines and foundries.

Luther in discussion with Bible scholars

Luther's childhood was one of serious piety and rigorous discipline. At age five Martin enrolled at the local Latin day school. At age thirteen he was sent to Magdeburg to a school conducted by the Brethren of the Common Life. At age fourteen he transferred to a school at Eisenach, where he had relatives. At age eighteen he began studies at the University of Erfurt. At age nineteen he received his baccalaureate (B.A.) and immediately began studies toward the masters degree. At age twenty-one he passed the exams (M.A.) after the shortest possible period of study, being second in his class. Very soon he began the study of Law, a decision probably influenced by his father. A number of God-ordained factors interrupted his legal studies and culminated in Luther's call to the ministry: Strict religious upbringing, a natural bent toward piety, recent experiences at the university, a severe self-inflicted accidental wound to the artery in his thigh at age nineteen, and the several weeks of recuperation and meditation, the sudden death of a close friend, Alexis, the plague which struck Erfurt ---all of these made Luther keenly aware of the preeminence of death. One additional "natural" calamity during Luther's twenty-second year produced the immediate flash point for Luther's decision to dedicate himself to the priesthood. In July 1505 while returning to Erfurt from a visit to his parents at Mansfield, "he encountered a severe thunderstorm near the village of Stotternheim. As a lightning bolt threw him to the ground, he vowed to St. Anne in a sudden panic that he would become a monk." [1] He later wrote: "not freely or desirously did I become a monk, but walled around with the terror and agony of sudden death, I vowed a constrained and necessary vow." [2]

Luther ordained to the ministry

Luther entered the Augustinian monastery at Erfurt on July 17, 1505, one of over two thousand such chapters. Ordained a priest April, 1507, at age twenty-three, Luther conducted his first mass in early May, 1507, attended by his father and some friends. He soon became the chair of moral philosophy in the arts faculty while continuing his studies at the University of Wittenberg. Late during the year of 1510 at age twenty-seven, Luther was selected to accompany Johann von Staupitz, vicar-general of the Saxon congregation of the Augustinians, to Rome, where he apparently spent a month visiting shrines and churches, and observing the very center of life of the Roman Catholic Church. He later wrote that he had encountered a horde of unlettered clergy whose "priests said Mass in such an irreverent fashion that it reminded him of a juggling act." [3] Luther's "earnestness was shocked by the levity of the Roman clergy and by the worldliness so evident in high places." [4]

With much encouragement from Staupitz, Luther completed the Doctor of Theology October 19, 1512 (shortly before his twenty-ninth birthday) and became a professor of biblical theology. "This was his lifelong calling, and the exposition of the Bible to his students was a task that called forth his best gifts and energies, one that he sustained until ill health and old age made him relinquish at the end of his life.

In between lectures, in a manner of speaking, he began the Protestant Reformation." [5]

Luther preaching at Wittenberg

Soon Luther succeeded Staupitz in the chair of Biblical Theology. God, however, had been at work in Luther's spirit, soul, and conscience. Luther bore a crippling burden of guilt. He later wrote "For however irreproachably I lived as a monk, I felt myself in the presence of God to be a sinner with a most unquiet conscience... I did not love, indeed I hated this just God...." [6] "He was increasingly conscious of the power of sin, and repeated confession brought him no peace... There were times when he felt on the brink of hell and the verge of despair. He tells us that while contemplating the righteousness of God in the monastery tower, probably in 1512 [age twenty-eight], a new concept, a new illumination came to him, and 'the gates of paradise were opened.'" [7]

"At last I began to understand the justice of God as that by which the just man lives by the gift of God..." [8] "For justification, no longer an objective transformation, is produced by the word of God, the Gospel. It is in, with, and through the Gospel that God works upon the soul through His Spirit. The soul remains passive and receptive like a woman in the act of conception. Thus Luther made an extremely personal experience the center of a new theology of salvation that was no longer in harmony with the one traditionally taught by the Church." [9] It was a divinely orchestrated series of events which caused Luther's spiritual struggles to spread far beyond the confines of his life and classroom and to change the course of history.

In 1514 Luther began as pastor in a local parish church. A year later he became district vicar over eleven other houses. In early 1517 Luther penned a series of theses against the Scholastic theologians, which he offered to defend at other universities, but had no takers. All of this prepared him for his best-known writing — *The Ninety-Five Theses* — written later in that same year.

The immediate catalysts which moved Luther to action were the St. Peter's Indulgence sale throughout Germany under the principal agent, Dominican Johann Tetzel, and the absolutely unbiblical teachings regarding pardon for sins through the giving of funds to the church as well as numerous other associated undeniable doctrinal errors. As Luther wrote *The Ninety-Five Theses* he was reacting to the indulgences, but chose to go far beyond their immediate concern and to put in writing some of his developing convictions regarding the essentials of the true Christian life and experience. He posted the *Theses* on the door of the Wittenberg church intending to hold a debate on the value of indulgences. It was the recent invention of the printing press (c. 1450) and a wide circulation of the *Theses* which turned Luther's writing from what might have been a local church squabble into an ever-widening public and national controversy.

Karlstadt responded with four hundred five theses. Luther published a bold sermon on the power of excommunication questioning the pope's seemingly unlimited power. Luther was summoned to Rome to defend himself. Luther met with Cardinal Cajetan, to whom he apologized for certain attitudes and actions, but did not recant. In 1520, at age thirty-seven, Luther wrote a series of pamphlets, *An Appeal to the Nobility of the German Nation*, *On the Babylonian Captivity of the Church*, and *Liberty of the Christian Man*. In January, 1521, the pope issued Luther's formal excommunication from the church and banned his writings.

Shortly thereafter Luther was secretly taken to Wartburg Castle where he spent a year in hiding. While there he produced a number of important writings, the chief of which was the beginning of his translation of the Holy Scriptures from the original Greek and Hebrew into the German vernacular which eventually had a deep and lasting influence on the language, life, and religion of Germany.

Desiderius Erasmus

In September, 1524, after much pressure from various sources, Desiderius Erasmus, a former Augustinian monk, and great liberal humanist, published his *Diatribe* (Discussion) *Concerning Free Will*, which was essentially an attack upon Luther's central doctrine regarding the Gospel of Salvation. In December, 1525, at age forty-two, Luther published his lengthy (four times as voluminous as Erasmus) response in his *Bondage of the Will*.

In June of the same year, probably while working on **Bondage**, Luther married Katherina von Bora, a former nun. She bore him six children, four of whom survived their parents. Martin and Katherina also raised eleven orphans.

Katherina von Bora

During his most influential years, Luther endeavored with all his strength to deal appropriately with Catholic church error, the radical and fanatical reformists, and the peasants who, during several periods, arose against their overlords. He was consistently against radicalism and violence as a means of reform, but rather insisted that the only true reform agent must be the **Word of God.** He taught one's duty of civil obedience and the sinfulness of rebellion against lawful authority.

Fittingly, perhaps, Luther died as a result of applying his godly wisdom, and his zeal for peace through biblical conciliation. Early in 1546, at age sixty-two, he was asked to mediate a quarrel between two arrogant young princes, Counts Albrecht and Gebhard of Mansfield. Old and ill, he accomplished the mission but overtaxed his strength and in a few hours died in Eisleben, the town of his birth on February 18, 1546. His body was interred in the Church of All Saints, Wittenberg.

During his lifetime Luther produced 400 works (100 volumes).

INTRODUCTION

A great many things about what is called "Evangelical Christianity" have changed in the five hundred years since Luther wrote. Instead of a few branches in the tree called Christianity, we now have hundreds. Each of these is not without significance to certain groups of followers. Each has chosen, for its own reasons, to emphasize certain aspects of what it holds to be *Christian truth*. Some branches seem to major in major doctrinal points, while others seem to emphasize minor points. Each defines in its own way, more or less, what the "ideal" or "perfect" Christian life should look like.

What is a Christian? What is a believer? What is a true believer? Are you a believer? Is your name written in the Lamb's Book of Life? Do you have the absolute assurance that when you pass from this life you will enter heaven to spend eternity with Jesus Christ and with all those of all the ages who have loved him and served him?

How did you become a Christian? Was it through baptism? Was it a result of a decision you once made in response to the preaching of the gospel? Was it an emotional thing? Was it at a Billy Graham meeting, or even perhaps at a "Christian Rock Concert?" Was your conversion a sudden thing, or did it occur over a period of days, or weeks? Can you point to a specific time when you became a believer in Jesus?

This book will seek to clarify for every person who has named the name of Christ, some basic truths about salvation which one cannot ignore as one seeks to make his "calling and election sure." (2 Peter 1:10) I think the reader will agree that ultimately we come to God on *His terms*, not ours. It is my strong belief that many who have begun the Christian walk have done so with very little understanding of what "being saved" means from God's perspective. This book will help the believer to clarify that aspect of salvation. It will also help the believer to more fully understand the biblical truth that his own will and his own decision were not the key factors in his becoming a true believer. Let me begin with a simple anecdote which illustrates a great Biblical truth:

Do you know the current President of the United States of America? You will probably answer "Yes." But now answer this question: "Does the current President of the United States of America know you?" Very few readers would be able to answer "Yes" to this question. In the same line of thought, if I were to ask you:

"Do you know Jesus Christ?" I expect that you would answer "Yes." But if I ask you, "Does Jesus Christ know you?" what would your answer be? This is the crucial question of determining if you are truly born again, saved, and in a right relationship with God. You must *know* that *he* knows you.

Jesus made this very plain when he said:

"Not every one that saith unto me, Lord, Lord, shall enter into the kingdom of heaven; but he that doeth the will of my Father which is in heaven. Many will say to me in that day, Lord, Lord, have we not prophesied in thy name? and in thy name have cast out devils? and in thy name done many wonderful works? And then will I profess unto them, **I never knew you**: depart from me, ye that work iniquity. (Matthew 7:21-23 KJV)

Do you have the inner assurance that Jesus Christ knows you in a saving relationship? It is my goal that as a result of reading this book and coming to understand the great truths which Martin Luther wrote in what he considered his greatest work, *The Bondage of the Will*, you will come to understand in some wonderful new ways just how great is the salvation which Jesus Christ has purchased with his own blood.

Another way to look at the question is this: *Are you saved by an act of your will, or by an act of God's will?* In the author's experience most believers during the early part of their Christian life have a strong belief that it was their own doing, an act of their own will which caused them to become a believer. However, the Scriptures are very clear on this point. No one is saved by an act of his own will. All are saved by an act of God's will. In fact, there are two points at which God's will is active in your salvation: (1) God willed your salvation before the worlds were created (refs: Rev. 13:8; 17:8; Eph 1:4; 2 Thess 2:18), and (2) it was an act of God's will *in time* which caused your new birth (refs: John 3:8; Eph 1:11; Jas 1:18). In addition, God's will is evidenced by the fact that you are *chosen* (John 15:16,19; Eph 1:4; 2 Thess 2:13) and *elect* (Matt 24:24, 31; Mk 13:22,27; Rom 8:28-39; 1 Pet 1:1-5).

The primary focus of Martin Luther's writing in ***The Bondage of the Will*** is to answer the question: ***"Does man have free will?"*** The ultimate answer to the question comes down to this: Whose will is sovereign — God's or man's? If God wills a thing (such as a person's salvation) can that person thwart God's sovereign will? The logical and obvious answer is "No, no created being may thwart the will of the Creator."

In essence, an overview of what God has willed in His creation is that (1) the gospel of Jesus Christ is to be preached to every creature, (2) those whom God has chosen will believe, (3) those who believe are given, by God, the gifts of faith and grace by which they are empowered to believe. Without these gifts, because all men are dead in trespasses and sins, no man could ever believe. The Scriptures make very clear that God's way of salvation is all due to God's grace, and not one whit due to man's will or man's goodness — that no flesh should glory in His sight.

May this book clarify some very important basic biblical truths for you. May this book build you up in the faith. May this book assist you to come to a new understanding of the Holy Scriptures, as you read them and study them in the days and years to come — until He comes.

Martin Luther called them, as translated from the Latin, ***assertions***. I choose to call them ***theses***, because they follow the pattern of his ***Ninety-Five Theses***. They are statements of what Martin Luther believed as a Christian—and what he strongly asserts that every Christian should believe. As the reader will soon see, Martin Luther took the time to define what he meant by assertions, so the reader will have no doubt about what he meant.

Another good word would be ***convictions***. We live in a time when living lives based upon Biblical convictions has never been more sorely needed. May your reading and understanding of Martin Luther's assertions and the commentary contained herein bring blessing and honor to our Lord Jesus Christ as He works mightily in your life through this study.

Please note: All **bold-face** type is taken from the text of the complete book, and endnoted. **Numbered Superscript Endnotes** reference from where, in the original translated and edited 1823 Henry Cole text, the numbered section is taken. No actual accounting is made of the "450 Theses" originally counted by the current author/editor. All editing has been done to improve the clarity of Martin Luther's intent. **Footnotes** are used sparingly, and are also indicated with a superscript numeral [1] in the text. **Passages of the text which are double indented and more closely line-spaced are so formatted to add emphasis.** Chapter headings in boxes with brief summaries of the chapter have been added. Whenever the second person "you" or "your" is found in the text it is understood to refer to Erasmus, to whom the entire work was addressed. Let us here proceed to Martin Luther's four hundred fifty theses, convictions, or assertions.

CHAPTER 1:
ASSERTIONS, CONVICTIONS, THESES

Martin Luther begins the discussion by defining the importance of a Christian believer holding certain assertions or convictions regarding his faith, and of the importance of the believer speaking out and defending such assertions, which is the primary reason for his writing the present work.

1. For not to delight in assertions, is not the character of the Christian mind: no, he must delight in assertions, or he is not a Christian. But, (that we may not be mistaken in terms) by *assertion*, I mean a constant adhering, affirming, confessing, defending, and invincibly persevering.[10]

2. Nothing is more clearly known and more common among Christians than assertions. Take away assertions, and you take away Christianity. In fact, the Holy Spirit is given unto Christians from heaven, that He may glorify Christ, and confess Him even unto death. And the ultimate demonstration of assertion is to die for confession and assertion. [11]

3. The Christian will rather say this—I am so averse to the sentiments of the Sceptics, that wherever I am not hindered by the infirmity of the flesh, I will not only steadily adhere to the Sacred Writings everywhere, and in all parts of them, and assert them, but I wish also to be as certain as possible in things that are not essential, and that lie outside the Scripture; for what is more miserable than uncertainty. [12]

4. The Holy Spirit is not a Skeptic, nor are what he has written on our hearts doubts or opinions, but assertions more certain, and more firm, than life itself and all human experience. [13]

5. That there are in God many hidden things which we know not, no one doubts: as He himself says concerning the last day: "Of that day

knoweth no man but the Father." (Matt. 24:36.) And (Acts 1:7.) "It is not yours to know the times and seasons." And again, "I know whom I have chosen," (John 13:18.) And Paul, "The Lord knoweth them that are His," (2 Tim. 2:19.). And the like.

But, that there are in the Scriptures some things obscure, and that all things are not quite plain, is a report spread abroad by the impious Sophists – those cleaver, deceiving logic-choppers – by whose mouth you speak here, Erasmus. But they never have produced, nor ever can produce, one article whereby to prove this their madness. And it is with such scare-crows that Satan has frightened away men from reading the Sacred Writings, and has rendered the Holy Scripture contemptible, that he might cause his poisons of philosophy to prevail in the church. This indeed I confess, that there are many *places* in the Scriptures obscure and hard to understand; not from the majesty of the thing, but from our ignorance of certain terms and grammatical particulars; but which do not prevent a knowledge of all the *things* in the Scriptures. For what *thing* of more importance can remain hidden in the Scriptures, now that the seals are broken, the stone rolled from the door of the sepulcher, and that greatest of all mysteries brought to light, Christ made man: that God is Trinity and Unity: that Christ suffered for us, and will reign to all eternity? [14]

6. But to know that all things in the Scriptures are set in the clearest light, and then, because a few words are obscure, to report that the things are obscure, is absurd and impious. *And, if the words are obscure in one place, yet they are clear in another.* But, however, the same *thing*, which has been most openly declared to the whole world, is both spoken of in the Scriptures in plain words, and also still lies hidden in obscure words. Now, therefore, it matters not if the thing be in the light, whether any certain representations of it be in obscurity or not, if, in the mean while, many other representations of the same thing be in the light. [15]

7. But, if many things still remain obscure to many, this does not arise from obscurity in the Scriptures, but from their own blindness or lack of understanding, who do not or cannot discover the all-perfect clearness of the truth. As Paul says concerning the Jews, 2 Cor. 3:15. "The veil still remains upon their heart." And again, "If our gospel be hid it is hid to them that are lost, whose heart the god of this world hath blinded." (2 Cor. 4:3-4.) With the same rashness anyone may cover his own eyes, or go from the light into the dark and hide himself, and then blame the day and the sun for being obscure. [16]

8. Isaiah 40:13, does not say, Who has known the mind of the Scripture, but, who has known "the mind of the Lord?" Although Paul asserts that the mind of the Lord is known to Christians: but it is in those things which are freely given unto us: as he says also in the same place, 1 Cor. 2:10, 16. [17]

9. It is not irreligious, strange, or excessive, but essentially wholesome and necessary, for a Christian to know, whether or not the will does anything in those things which pertain unto Salvation. Nay, let me tell you, this is the very hinge upon which our discussion turns. It is the very heart of our subject. For our object is this: to inquire what "Freewill" can do, in what it is passive, and how it stands with reference to the grace of God. *If we know nothing of these things, we shall know nothing whatever of Christian matters, and shall be far behind all People upon the earth.* He that does not feel this, let him confess that he is no Christian. And he that despises and laughs at it, let him know that he is the Christian's greatest enemy. For, if I know not how much I can do myself, how far my ability extends, and what I can do toward God; I shall be equally uncertain and ignorant how much God is to do, how far His ability is to extend, and what He is to do toward me: whereas it is "God that worketh all in all." (1 Cor. 12:6.) But if I know not the distinction between our working and the power of God, I know not God

Himself. And if I know not God, I cannot worship Him, praise Him, give Him thanks, nor serve Him; for I shall not know how much I ought to ascribe unto myself, and how much unto God. It is necessary, therefore, to hold the most certain distinction, between the power of God and our power, the working of God and our working, if we would live in proper holy fear toward Him. [18]

10. We owe much to you [Erasmus], but we owe all to the fear of God. Nay you yourself see, that all our good is to be ascribed unto God, and you assert that in your Form of Christianity: and in asserting this, you certainly, at the same time assert also, that the mercy of God alone does all things, and that our own will does nothing, but is rather acted upon: and so it must be, otherwise the whole is not ascribed unto God. [19]

11. THIS, therefore, is also essentially necessary and wholesome for Christians to know: *That God foreknows nothing by contingency, but that He foresees, purposes, and does all things according to His immutable, eternal, and infallible will.* By this thunderbolt, "Freewill" is thrown prostrate, and utterly dashed to pieces. Those, therefore, who would assert "Freewill," must either deny this thunderbolt, or pretend not to see it, or push it from them. [20]

12. If then, He foreknows, willing, His will is eternal and immovable, because His nature is so: and, if He wills, foreknowing, His knowledge is eternal and immovable, because His nature is so. From which it follows unalterably, that all things which we do, although they may appear to us to be done mutably and contingently – that is, by our own free and unhindered choice – and even may be done thus contingently – that is, after we have considered, more or less, the various choices which are set before us – by us, are yet, in reality, done necessarily and immutably, with respect to the will of God. For the will of God is effective and cannot be hindered; because the very power of God is

natural to Him, and His wisdom is such that He cannot be deceived. And as His will cannot be hindered, the work itself cannot be hindered from being done in the place, at the time, in the measure, and by whom He foresees and wills. If the will of God were such, that, when the *work* was done, the *work* remained but the *will* ceased, (as is the case with the *will* of men, which, when the house is built which they wished to build, ceases to *will*, as though it ended by death) then, indeed, it might be said, that things are done by contingency and mutability. But here, the case is the contrary; the *work ceases,* and the *will remains.* So far is it from possibility, that the doing of the work or its remaining, can be said to be from contingency or mutability. But, (that we may not be deceived in terms) *being done by contingency,* does not, in the Latin language, signify that the work itself which is done is contingent, but that it is done according to a contingent and mutable will—such a will as is not to be found in God! Moreover, a work cannot be called contingent, unless it be done by us unawares, by contingency, and, as it were, by chance; that is, by our will or hand catching at it, as presented by chance,we thinking nothing of it,nor willing anything about it before.[21]

13. The will, whether divine or human, does what it does, be it good or evil, not by any compulsion but by mere willingness or desire, as it were, totally free. The will of God, nevertheless, which rules over our mutable will, is immutable and infallible; as Boetius sings, "Immovable Thyself, Thou movement giv'st to all." And our own will, especially our corrupt will, cannot of itself do good; therefore, where the term fails to express the idea required, the understanding of the reader must make up the deficiency, knowing what is wished to be expressed—the immutable will of God, and the impotency of our depraved will. . ." [22]

14. This asserted truth, therefore, stands and remains invincible—that all things take place according to the immutable will of God! which they call the necessity of the consequence. Nor is there here any obscurity or

ambiguity. In Isaiah he says, "My counsel shall stand, and My will shall be done." (Isa. 46:10.) And what schoolboy does not understand the meaning of these expressions, "Counsel," "will," "shall be done," "shall stand?" [23]

15. For if you doubt, or disdain to know that God foreknows and wills all things, not contingently, but necessarily and immutably, how can you believe confidently, trust in, and depend upon His promises? For when He promises, it is necessary that you should be certain that He knows, is able, and willing to perform what He promises; otherwise, you will neither hold Him true nor faithful; which is unbelief, the greatest of wickedness, and a denying of the Most High God!

And how can you be certain and secure, unless you are persuaded that He knows and wills certainly, infallibly, immutably, and necessarily, and will perform what He promises? Nor ought we to be certain only that God wills necessarily and immutably, and will perform, but also to glory in the same; as Paul, (Rom. 3:4,) "Let God be true, but every man a liar." And again, "For the Word of God is not without effect." (Rom. 9:6.) And in another place, "The foundation of God standeth sure, having this seal, the Lord knoweth them that are His." (2 Tim. 2:19.) And, "Which God, that cannot lie, promised before the world began." (Titus 1:2.) And, "He that cometh, must believe that God is, and that He is a rewarder of them that hope in Him." (Heb. 11:6) [24]

16. The greatest and only consolation of Christians in their adversities, is the sure knowledge that God lies not, but does all things immutably, and that His will cannot be resisted, changed, or hindered. [25]

17. As I have said before, those things which are either found in the sacred Writings, or may be proved by them, are not only plain, but wholesome; and therefore may be, nay, ought to be, spread abroad,

learned, and known. [26]

18. I confess indeed, that there are certain delusive preachers, who, not from any religion, or fear of God, but from a desire of vainglory, or from a thirst after some novelty, or from impatience of silence, babble and trifle in the lightest manner. But such please neither God nor men, although they assert that God is in the Heaven of Heavens. But when there are sober and pious preachers, who teach in modest, pure, and sound words; they, without any danger, nay, unto much profit, speak on such a subject before the multitude.

Is it not the duty of us all to teach, that the Son of God was in the womb of the Virgin, and proceeded forth from her belly? And in what does the human womb differ from any other unclean place? Who, moreover, may not describe it in unpleasant and shameless terms? But such persons we justly condemn; because, there are countless pure words, in which we speak of that necessary subject, even with decency and grace. The body also of Christ Himself was human, like ours. What is more filthy than a mortal human body? But shall we, therefore, not say what Paul says, that God dwelt in it bodily? (Col. 2:9.) What is more unclean than death? What more horrible than hell? Yet the prophet glories that God was with Christ in death, and left Him not in hell. (Ps. 16:10, Ps. 139:8). [27]

19. A good theologian teaches that the common people are to be restrained by the external power of the sword, where they do evil: as Paul teaches. (Rom. 13:1-4.) But their consciences are not to be shackled by false laws, that they might be tormented with sins where God wills there should be no sins at all. For consciences are bound by the Law of God only. So that, that intermediate tyranny of Popes, which falsely terrifies and murders the people's spirits, and vainly wearies their bodies, is to be taken entirely out of the way. Because, although it binds to confession and other things, outwardly, yet the mind is not, by these

things restrained, but exasperated the more into the hatred both of God and men. And in vain does it butcher the body by external things, making nothing but hypocrites.—So that tyrants, with laws of this kind, are nothing else but ravening wolves, robbers, and plunderers of souls.[28]

20. I am, in this discussion, seeking an object solemn and essential; nay, such, and so great, that it ought to be maintained and defended through death itself; and that, although the whole world should not only be thrown into tumult and set in arms thereby, but even if it should be hurled into chaos and reduced to nothing. [29]

21. If we put off the infallible Word of God, we put off God, faith, salvation and all Christianity together. How far different from this is the instruction of Christ: that, we should rather despise the whole world!

BUT you say these things, because you either do not read or do not observe, that such is most constantly the case with the Word of God, that because of it, the world is thrown into tumult. And that Christ openly declares: "I came not (says He) to send peace but a sword." (Matt. 10:34.) And in Luke, "I came to send fire upon the earth." (Luke 12:49.) And Paul, (2 Cor. 6:5,) "In tumults,". . . And the Prophet, in the Second Psalm, abundantly testifies the same: declaring, that the nations are in tumult, the people roaring, the kings rising up, and the princes conspiring against the Lord and against His Christ. As though He had said, multitude, height, wealth, power, wisdom, righteousness, and whatever is great in the world, sets itself against the Word of God.

Look into the Acts of the Apostles, and see what happened in the world on account of the word of Paul only (to say nothing of the other apostles): how he alone throws both the Gentiles and Jews into uproar: or, as the enemies themselves express it, "turns the world upside down." (Acts 17:6.) Under Elijah, the kingdom of Israel was thrown into turmoil: as king Ahab complains. (1 Kings 18:17.) What tumult was there under the other prophets, while they are all either killed at once or stoned to death; while Israel is taken captive into Assyria, and Judah also to Babylon! Was all this peace? The world and its god (2 Cor. 4:4,) cannot and will not bear the Word of the true God: and the true God cannot and will not keep silence. While, therefore, these two Gods are at war with each other, what can there be else in the whole world, but tumult?

Therefore, to wish to silence these tumults, is nothing else, than to wish to hinder the Word of God, and to take it out of the way. For the Word of God, wherever it comes, comes to change and to renew the world. And even heathen writers testify, that changes of things cannot take place, without commotion and tumult, nor even without blood. It therefore belongs to Christians, to expect and endure these things, with a resolute mind: as Christ says, "When ye shall hear of wars and rumors of wars, be not dismayed, for these things must first come to pass, but the end is not yet." (Matt. 24:6.) And as to myself, if I did not see these tumults, I should say the Word of God was not in the world. But now, when I do see them, I rejoice from my heart, and fear them not: being surely persuaded, that the kingdom of the Pope, with all his followers, will fall to the ground: for it is especially against this, that the Word of God, which now runs, is directed. [30]

22. This tumult proceeds, and is carried on, from above, and will not cease until it shall make all the adversaries of the Word as the dirt of the streets. [31]

23. These things, I say, as they are temporal, are borne with less evil than chronic and evil habits; by which all souls must be destroyed if they are not changed by the Word of God: which being taken away, eternal good, God, Christ, and the Spirit, must be taken away with it.

But how much better is it to lose the whole world, than to lose God the Creator of the world, who can create innumerable worlds again, and is better than infinite worlds? For what are temporal things when compared with eternal? This leprosy of temporal things, therefore, is rather to be borne, than that every soul should be destroyed and eternally damned, and the world kept in peace, and preserved from these tumults, by their blood and eternal damnation: whereas, one soul cannot be redeemed with the price of the whole world! [32]

24. But I, by the grace of God, see these things clearly; because, I see other tumults greater than these that will arise in the age to come in comparison of which, these appear but as the whispering of a breath of air, or the murmuring of a gentle brook. [33]

25. But we know, and are persuaded, that there is a Word of God, in which the Christian liberty is asserted, that we might not allow ourselves to be ensnared into bondage by human traditions and laws. [34]

26. The prince of this world will not allow the Pope and his high priests, and their laws to be observed in liberty, but his design is to entangle and bind consciences. This the true God will not bear. Therefore, the Word of God, and the traditions of men, are opposed to each other with implacable discord; no less so, than God Himself and Satan; who each destroy the works and overthrow the doctrines of the other, as regal kings each destroying the kingdom of the other. "He that is not with Me (says Christ) is against Me." (Luke 11:23.) [35]

27. Was not the world always drowned in war, fraud, violence, discord, and every kind of iniquity? For if Micah (7:4) compares the best among them to a thorn hedge, what do you suppose he would call the rest? But now that the Gospel is come, men begin to impute unto it, that the world is evil. Whereas, the truth is, that by the good Gospel, it is more mani-fest how evil it was, while, without the Gospel, it did all its works in

darkness. Thus also the illiterate attribute it to learning, that, by its flourishing, their ignorance becomes known. This is the return we make for the Word of life and salvation!—And what fear must we suppose there was among the Jews, when the Gospel freed all from the Law of Moses? What occasion did not this great liberty seem to give to evil men? But yet, the Gospel was not, on that account, taken away; but the impious were left, and it was preached to the pious, that they might not use their liberty to an occasion of the flesh. (Gal. 5:13.) [36]

28. Truth and doctrine, are to be preached always, openly, and firmly, and are never to be dissembled or concealed; for there is no offense in them; they are the staff of uprightness. [37]

29. Nor did God give us the Word that it should be had with respect of places, persons, or times: for Christ says, "Go ye out into the whole world,": He does not say, as Erasmus does,—go to this place and not to that. Again, "Preach the Gospel to every creature." (Mark 16:15) He does not say—preach it to some and not to others. In a word, you enjoin, in the administration of the Word of God, a respect of persons, a respect of places, a respect of customs, and a respect of times: whereas, the one and especial part of the glory of the Word consists in this,—that, as Paul says, there is, with it, no respect of persons; and that God is no respecter of persons. [38]

30. How much better is it for us wretched men to ascribe unto God, who knows the hearts of all men, the glory of determining the manner in which, the persons to whom, and the times in which the truth is to be spoken. For He knows what is to be spoken to each, and when, and how it is to be spoken. He then, determines that His Gospel which is necessary unto all, should be confined to no place, no time; but that it should be preached unto all, at all times and in all places. [39]

31. I tell you again, that human statutes cannot be observed together with the Word of God: because, the former bind consciences, the latter looses them. They are directly opposed to each other, as water to fire. Unless, indeed, they could be observed in liberty; that is, not to bind the conscience. [40]

32. The authority of the church fathers, therefore, is to be accounted nothing: and those statutes which have been wrongly enacted, (as all have been that are not according to the Word of God) are to be torn up and cast away: for Christ is better than the authority of the church fathers. [41]

33. What is more severe, that is, to the flesh, than that Word of Christ "Many are called but few chosen?" (Matt. 22:14) And again, "I know whom I have chosen?" (John 13:18). [42]

34. You well nigh frightened us from reading the Scriptures altogether; (to the reading of which Christ and His apostles urge and persuade us, as well as you do yourself elsewhere.) [43]

35. It is here the hand is to be laid upon the mouth, it is here we are to reverence what lies hidden, to adore the secret counsels of the divine Majesty, and to exclaim with Paul, "Who art thou, O man, that contendest with God?" (Rom. 9:20)

"WHO (you say) will endeavour to amend his life?"—I answer, No man! no man can! For your self-amenders without the Spirit, God regardeth not, for they are hypocrites. But the Elect, and those that fear God, will be amended by the Holy Spirit; the rest will perish unamended. Nor does Augustine say, that the works of *none*, nor that the works *of all* are crowned, but the works *of some*. Therefore, there will be *some*, who shall amend their lives.

"Who will believe (you say) that he is loved of God?"—I answer, no man will believe it! No man can! But the Elect shall believe it; the rest shall perish without believing it, filled with indignation and blaspheming, as you here describe them. Therefore, there will be *some* who shall believe it.

And as to your saying that—"by these doctrines the flood-gate of iniquity is thrown open unto men"—be it so. They pertain to that leprosy of evil to be borne, spoken of before. Nevertheless, by the same doctrines, there is thrown open to the Elect and to them that fear God, a gate unto righteousness,—an entrance into heaven—a way unto God! But if, according to your advice, we would refrain from these doctrines, and would hide from men this Word of God, so that each, deluded by a false persuasion of salvation, would never learn to fear God, and would never be humbled, in order that through this fear he might come to grace and love; then, indeed, we would shut up your flood-gate on purpose! For in the place of it, we would throw open to ourselves and to all, wide gates, nay, yawning chasms and sweeping tides, not only unto iniquity, but unto the depths of hell! Thus, we would not enter into Heaven ourselves, and them that were entering in we would hinder.

"What utility therefore (you say) is there in, or necessity for proclaiming such things openly, when so many evils seem likely to proceed therefrom?"

I answer. It were enough to say—God has willed that they should be proclaimed openly: but the reason of the divine will is not to be inquired into, but simply to be adored, and the glory to be given unto God: who, since He alone is just and wise, does evil to no one, and can do nothing rashly or inconsiderately, although it may appear far otherwise unto us. With this answer those that fear God are content. But that, from the abundance of answering issues which I have, I may say a little more than this, which might suffice;—there are two causes which require such things to be preached. The first is, the humbling of our pride, and the knowledge of the grace of God. The second is, Christian faith itself.

First, God has promised certainly His grace to the humbled: that is, to the self-deploring and despairing. But a man cannot be thoroughly humbled, until he comes to know that his salvation is utterly beyond his own powers, counsel, endeavours, will, and works, and absolutely depending on the will, counsel, pleasure, and work of another, that is, of God only. For if, as long as he has any persuasion that he can do even the least thing himself towards his own salvation, he retains a confidence in himself and does not utterly despair in himself, so long he is not humbled before God; but he proposes to himself some place, some time, or some work, whereby he may at length attain unto salvation. But he who hesitates not to depend wholly upon the goodwill of God, he totally despairs in himself, chooses nothing for himself, but waits for God to work in him; and such an one, is the nearest unto grace, that he might be saved.

These things, therefore, are openly proclaimed for the sake of the Elect: that, being by these means humbled and brought down to nothing, they might be saved. The rest resist this humiliation; nay, they condemn the teaching of self-desperation; they wish to have left a little something that they may do themselves. These secretly remain proud, and adversaries to the grace of God. This, I say, is one reason—that those who fear God, being humbled, might know, call upon, and receive the grace of God.

The other reason is—that faith is, in *things not seen*. Therefore, that there might be room for faith, it is necessary that all those things which are believed should be hidden. But they are not hidden more deeply than under the contrary of sight, sense, and experience. Thus, when God makes alive, He does it by killing; when He justifies, He does it by bringing in a guilty verdict: when He exalts to Heaven, He does it by bringing down to hell: as the Scripture says, "The Lord killeth and maketh alive, He bringeth down to the grave and raiseth up, " (1 Sam. 2:6); concerning which, there is no need that I should here speak more at large, for those who read my writings, are well acquainted with these things. Thus He conceals His eternal mercy and loving-kindness behind

His eternal wrath: His righteousness, behind apparent iniquity.

This is the highest degree of faith—to believe that He is merciful, who saves so few and damns so many; to believe Him just, who according to His own will, makes us necessarily damnable, that He may seem, as Erasmus says, 'to delight in the torments of the miserable, and to be an object of hatred rather than of love.' If, therefore, I could by any means comprehend how that same God can be merciful and just, who carries the appearance of so much wrath and iniquity, there would be no need of faith. But now, since that cannot be comprehended, there is room for exercising faith, while such things are preached and openly proclaimed: in the same manner as, while God kills, the faith of life is exercised in death. [44]

36. AS to the other paradox you mention,—that, 'whatever is done by us, is not done by Freewill, but from mere necessity'—

Let us briefly consider this, lest we should allow anything most malevolently spoken, to pass by unnoticed. Here then, I observe, that if it be proved that our salvation is apart from our own strength and counsel, and depends on the working of God alone, (which I hope I shall clearly prove hereafter, in the course of this discussion,) does it not evidently follow, that when God is not present with us to work in us, every thing that we do is evil, and that we of necessity do those things which are of no avail unto salvation? For if it is not we ourselves, but God only, that works salvation in us, it must follow, logically, that we do nothing unto salvation *before* the working of God in us.

But, by *necessity*, I do not mean *compulsion*; but (as they term it) the *necessity of immutability*, not of *compulsion*; that is, a man void of the Spirit of God, does not do evil against his will as by violence, or as if he were taken by the neck and forced to it, in the same way as a thief or cut-throat is dragged to punishment against his will; but he does it spontaneously, and with a desirous willingness. And this willingness and desire of doing evil he cannot, by his own power, leave off, restrain, or change; but it goes on still desiring and craving. And even if he should be compelled by force to do anything *outwardly* to the contrary, yet the craving will *within* remains averse to, and rises in indignation against that which forces or resists it. But it would not rise in indignation, if it were changed, and made willing to yield to a constraining power. This is what we mean by the necessity of immutability:—that the will cannot change itself, nor give itself another bent; but rather the more it is resisted, the more it is irritated to crave; as is manifest from its indignation. This would not be the case if it were free, or had a "Freewill." Ask experience, how hardened against all persuasion they are, whose inclinations are fixed upon any one thing. For if they yield at all, they yield through force, or through something attended with greater advantage; they never yield willingly. And if their inclinations be not thus fixed, they let all things pass and go on just as they will.

But again, on the other hand, when God works in us, the *will*, being changed and sweetly breathed on by the Spirit of God, desires and acts, not from *compulsion*, but *responsively*, from pure willingness, inclination, and accord; so that it cannot be turned another way by anything contrary, nor be compelled or overcome even by the gates of hell; but it still goes on to desire, crave after, and love that which is good; even as before, it desired, craved after, and loved that which was evil. This, again, experience proves. How invincible and unshaken are holy men, when, by violence and other oppressions, they are only compelled and irritated the more to crave after good! Even as fire is rather fanned into flames than extinguished, by the wind. So that neither is there here any willingness, or "Freewill," to turn itself into another direction, or to desire anything else, while the influence of the Spirit and grace of God remain in the man.

In a word, if we be under the god of this world, without the operation and Spirit of God, we are led captives by him at his will, as Paul says. (2 Tim. 2:26) So that, we cannot will anything but that which he wills. For he is that "strong man armed," who so keepeth his palace, that those whom he holds captive are kept in peace, that they might not cause any motion or feeling against him; otherwise, the kingdom of Satan, being divided against itself, could not stand; whereas, Christ affirms it does stand. And all this we do willingly and desiringly, according to the nature of *will*: for if it were forced, it would be no longer *will*. For compulsion is (so to speak) *unwillingness*. But if the "stronger than he" come and overcome him, and take us as His spoils, then, through the Spirit, we are His servants and captives (which is the royal liberty) that we may desire and do, willingly, what He wills.

Thus the human will is, as it were, a beast between the two. If God sit thereon, it wills and goes where God will: as the Psalm says, "I am become as it were a beast before thee, and I am continually with thee." (Ps. 73:22-23) If Satan sit thereon, it wills and goes as Satan will. Nor is it in the power of its own will to choose, to which rider it will run, nor which it will seek; but the riders themselves contend, which of them shall have and hold it. [45]

37. And hence it follows, that "Freewill," without the grace of God is, absolutely, not FREE; but, immutably, the servant and bond-slave of evil; because, it cannot turn itself unto good. [46]

38. But if we call the power of "Freewill" that, by which a man is fitted to be caught by the Spirit, or to be touched by the grace of God, as one created unto eternal life or eternal death, may be said to be; this power, that is, fitness, or, (as the Sophists term it) 'disposition-quality,' and 'passive aptitude,' this I also confess. And who does not know that this is not in trees or animals? For, (as they say) Heaven was not made for geese.

Therefore, it stands confirmed, even by your own testimony, that we do all things from necessity, not from "Freewill:" seeing that, the power of "Freewill" is nothing, and neither does, nor can do good, without grace. [47]

**39. It then follows immediately, that Freewill is plainly a divine term,
and can be applicable to none but the divine Majesty only: for He alone
"does, (as the Psalm sings) what He will in Heaven and earth." (Ps.
135:6.) Whereas, if it be ascribed unto men, it is not more properly
ascribed, than the deity of God Himself would be ascribed unto them:
which would be the greatest of all sacrilege. Wherefore, it becomes
Theologians to refrain from the use of this term altogether, whenever
they wish to speak of human ability, and to leave it to be applied to God
only. And moreover, to take this same term out of the mouths and
speech of men; and thus to assert, as it were, for their God, that which
belongs to His own sacred and holy Name.**

**But if they must, whether or no, give some power to men, let them
teach, that it is to be called by some other term than "Freewill";
especially since we know and clearly see, that the people are miserably
deceived and seduced by that term, taking and understanding it to
signify something far different from that which Theologians mean and
understand by it, in their discussions. For the term, "Freewill," is by far
too grand, copious, and full: by which, the people imagine is signified
(as the force and nature of the term requires) that power, which can
freely turn itself as it will, and such a power as is under the influence of,
and subject to no one. Whereas, if they knew that it was quite otherwise,
and that by that term scarcely the least spark or degree of power was
signified, and that, utterly ineffective of itself, being the servant and
bond-slave of the devil, it would not be at all surprising if they should
stone us as mockers and deceivers, who said one thing and meant
something quite different; nay, who left it uncertain and unintelligible
what we meant. [48]**

**40. But here *[the false idea of "freewill]* is a peril of salvation, and the
most destructive mockery. [49]**

41. If we do not like to abandon this term *[Freewill]* altogether, (which

would be most safe, and also most religious) we may, nevertheless, with a good conscience teach, that it be used so far as to allow man a "Freewill," not in respect of those which are above him, but in respect only of those things which are below him: that is, he may be allowed to know, that he has, as to his goods and possessions the right of using, acting, and omitting, according to his "Freewill;" although, at the same time, that same "Freewill" is overruled by the Freewill of God alone, just as He pleases: but that, God-ward, or in things which pertain unto salvation or damnation, he has no "Freewill," but is a captive, slave, and servant, either to the will of God, or to the will of Satan. [50]

42. Nor have I undertaken this discussion for the purpose of commending myself, but that I might exalt the grace of God. What I am, and with what spirit and design I have been led to these things, I leave to Him who knows, that all this is proceeding according to his own Freewill, not according to mine: though even the world itself ought to have found that out already. [51]

43. There is an old proverb, "Many were accounted saints on earth, whose souls are now in hell!" [52]

44. And even if we should grant, that some of the Elect are held in error through the whole of their life; yet they must, of necessity, return into the way of truth before their death; for Christ says, (John 10:28) "No one shall pluck them out of My hand." [53]

45. And who, even now, dares to deny that God, under all these great men, (for you make mention of none but men in some high office, or of some great name,) was reserving to Himself a Church among the common people, and allowing all those to perish after the example of the kingdom of Israel? For it is peculiar to God, to restrain the elect of Israel, and to slay their fat ones: but, to preserve the outcasts and

remnant of Israel, (Ps. 78: 31; Isaiah 1:9, 10:20-22, 11:11-16). [54]

46. And who knows who are the people of God, when throughout the whole world, from its origin, the state of the church was always such, that those were called the people and saints of God who were not so while others among them, who were as outcasts, and were not called the people and saints of God, were the People and Saints of God? as is manifest in the histories of Cain and Abel, of Ishmael and Isaac, of Esau and Jacob.

Look again at the age of the Arians, when scarcely five Catholic bishops were preserved throughout the whole world, and they, driven from their places, while the Arians reigned, every where bearing the public name and office of the church. Nevertheless, under these heretics, Christ preserved His Church: but so, that it was the least thought or considered to be the Church.

Again, show me, under the kingdom of the Pope, one bishop discharging his office. Show me one council in which their transactions were concerning the things pertaining to godliness, and not rather, concerning gowns, dignities, revenues, and other baubles, which they could not say, without being mad, pertained to the Holy Spirit. Nevertheless they are called the church, when all, at least who live as they do, must be reprobates and anything but the church. And yet, even under them Christ preserved His Church, though it was not called the Church. How many Saints must you imagine those of the inquisition have, for some ages, burnt and killed, as John Huss and others, in whose time, no doubt, there lived many holy men of the same spirit!

Why do you not rather wonder at this, Erasmus, that there ever were, from the beginning of the world, more distinguished talents, greater erudition, more ardent pursuit among the world in general than among Christians or the people of God? As Christ Himself declares, "The children of this world are wiser than the children of light." (Luke 16:8) What Christian can be compared (to say nothing of the Greeks)

with Cicero alone for talents, for erudition, or for indefatigability? What shall we say, then, was the preventive cause that not one of them was able to attain unto grace, who certainly exerted "Freewill" with its utmost powers? Who dares say, that there was not one among them who contended for truth with all his efforts? And yet we must affirm that not one of them all attained unto it. Will you here too say, it is not to be believed, that God would utterly leave so many great men, throughout such a series of ages, and permit them to labor in vain? Certainly, if "Freewill" were any thing, or could do any thing, it must have appeared and wrought something in those men, at least in some one instance. But it availed nothing, nay it always wrought in the contrary direction. Hence by this argument only, it may be sufficiently proved, that "Freewill" is nothing at all, since no proof of it can be produced even from the beginning of the world to the end!

BUT to return—What wonder, if God should leave all the elders of the church to go their own ways, who thus permitted all the nations to go *their* own ways, as Paul says, Acts 14:16; 17:30?—But, my friend Erasmus, THE CHURCH OF GOD INDEED, IS NOT SO COMMON A THING AS THIS TERM, CHURCH OF GOD: NOR ARE THE SAINTS OF GOD INDEED, EVERY WHERE TO BE FOUND LIKE THE TERM, SAINTS OF GOD. THEY ARE PEARLS AND PRECIOUS JEWELS, WHICH THE SPIRIT DOES NOT CAST BEFORE SWINE; BUT WHICH, (AS THE SCRIPTURE EXPRESSES IT,) HE KEEPS HIDDEN, THAT THE WICKED SEE NOT THE GLORY OF GOD! Otherwise, if they were openly known of all, how could it come to pass that they should be thus vexed and afflicted in the world? As Paul says, (1 Cor. 2:8) "Had they known Him, they would not have crucified the Lord of glory."

I do not say these things, because I deny that those whom you mention are the saints and church of God; but because it cannot be proved, if anyone should deny it, that they really are saints, but must be left quite in uncertainty; and because, therefore, the position deduced from their holiness, is not sufficiently credible for the confirmation of my doctrine. I call them saints, and look upon them as such: I call them the church, and look upon them as such—according to the Law of Charity, but not according to the Law of Faith. That is, charity, which always thinks the best of every one, and suspects not, but believes and presumes all things for good concerning its neighbour, calls every one who is baptized, a saint. Nor is there any peril if she err, for charity is liable to err; seeing that she is exposed to all the uses and abuses of all; an universal handmaid, to the good and to the evil, to the believing and to the unbelieving, to the true and to the false.—But faith, calls no one a saint but him who is declared to be so by the judgment of God, for faith is not liable to be deceived. Therefore, although we ought all to be looked upon as saints by each other by the Law of charity, yet no one ought to be decreed a saint by the Law of faith, so as to make it an article of faith that such or such an one is a Saint. For in this way, that adversary of God, the Pope, canonized his minions whom he knows not to be saints, setting himself in the place of God. (2 Thess. 2:4) [55]

Martin Luther with his family

CHAPTER 2:

ARE THE SCRIPTURES OBSCURE OR CLEAR?

In opposition to the diabolical doctrine held by the Church of Rome that the Scriptures are hard to understand and that therefore the believer must depend upon "the interpreting Spirit" of the Pope, Luther shows, quoting numerous Scriptures as well as giving a number of common sense examples of the great truth of holding to and teaching the concept that the Scriptures are full of light.

47. For we shall not search out the Spirit by the arguments of scholarship, of life, of talent, of multitude, of dignity, of ignorance, of inexperience, of scarcity of knowledge, or of meanness of rank. And yet, I do not approve of those, whose whole resource is in a boasting of the Spirit. For I had the last year, and have still, a sharp disagreement with those fanatics who subject the Scriptures to the interpretation of their own boastful spirit. On the same account also, I have heretofore determinately set myself against the Pope, in whose kingdom, nothing is more common, or more generally received than this saying:—'that the Scriptures are obscure and ambiguous, and that the Spirit, as the Interpreter, should be sought from the apostolic see of Rome!' Nothing could be said that was more destructive; for by means of this saying, a set of impious men have exalted themselves above the Scriptures themselves; and by the same, have done whatever pleased them; till at length, the Scriptures are absolutely trodden under foot, and we compelled to believe and teach nothing but the dreams of men that are mad. In a word, that saying is no human invention, but a poison poured forth into the world by a diabolical malice of the devil himself, the prince of all demons.

We hold the case thus:—that the spirits are to be tried and proved by a twofold judgment. The one, internal; by which, through the Holy

Spirit, or a special gift of God, anyone may illustrate, and to a certainty, judge of, and determine on, the doctrines and sentiments of all men, for himself and his own personal salvation concerning which it is said: (1 Cor. 2:15) "The spiritual man judgeth all things, but he himself is judged by no man." This belongs to faith, and is necessary for every Christian at every level of spiritual maturity. This, we have above called, 'the internal clearness of the Holy Scripture.' And it was this perhaps to which *they* alluded, who, in answer to you said, that all things must be determined by the judgment of the Spirit. But this judgment cannot profit another, nor are we speaking of this judgment in our present discussion; for no one, I think, doubts its reality.

The other, then, is the external judgment; by which, we judge, to the greatest certainty, of the spirits and doctrines of all men; not for ourselves only, but for others also, and for their salvation. This judgment is peculiar to the public ministry of the Word and the external office, and especially belongs to teachers and preachers of the Word. Of this we make use, when we strengthen the weak in faith, and when we refute adversaries. This is what we before called, 'the external clearness of the Holy Scripture.' Hence we affirm that all spirits are to be proved in the face of the church, by the judgment of Scripture.

> For this ought to be received, more than all things, and most
> firmly settled among Christians:—that the Holy Scriptures are
> a spiritual light by far more clear than the sun itself, especially
> in those things which pertain unto salvation or necessity.

BUT, since we have been persuaded to the contrary of this, by that pestilent saying of the Sophists, 'the Scriptures are obscure and ambiguous;' we are compelled, first of all, to prove that first grand principle of ours, by which all other things are to be proved: which, among the Sophists, is considered absurd and impossible to be done. First then, Moses says, (Deut. 17:8) that, 'if there arise a matter too hard in judgment, men are to go to the place which God shall choose for His name, and there to consult the priests, who are to judge of it according to the Law of the Lord.'

He says, "according to the Law of the Lord"—but how will they judge thus, if the Law of the Lord be not externally most clear, so as to satisfy them concerning it? Otherwise, it would have been sufficient, if he had said, according to their own spirit. Nay, it is so in every government of the people, the causes of all are settled according to laws. But how could they be settled, if the laws were not most certain, and absolutely true lights to the people? But if the laws were ambiguous and uncertain, there would not only be no causes settled, but no certain consistency of right behavior. Since, therefore, laws are enacted that good moral behavior may be regulated according to a certain form, and questions in causes settled, it is necessary that that, which is to be the rule and standard for men in their dealings with each other, as the law is, should of all things be the most certain and most clear. And if that light and certainty in laws, in earthly administrations where temporal things only are concerned, are necessary, and have been, by the goodness of God, freely granted to the whole world; how shall He not have given to Christians, that is, to His own Elect, laws and rules of much greater light and certainty, according to which they might adjust and settle both themselves and all their causes? And that more especially, since He wills that all temporal things should, by *His*, be despised. And "if God so clothe the grass of the field, which today is, and tomorrow is cast into the oven," how much more shall He clothe us? (Matt. 6:30)—But, let us proceed, and drown that pestilent saying of the Sophists, in Scriptures.

Psalm 19: 8, says, "The commandment of the Lord is clear (or pure), enlightening the eyes." And surely, that which enlightens the eyes, cannot be obscure or ambiguous!

Again, Psalm 119:130, "The door of thy words giveth light; it giveth understanding to the simple." Here, it is ascribed unto the words of God, that they are a door, and something open, which is quite plain to all and enlightens even the simple.

Isaiah 8:20, sends all questions "to the Law and to the testimony;"and threatens that if we do not do this, the light of the east shall be denied us.

In Malachi, 2:7, commands, 'that they should seek the Law from the mouth of the priest, as being the messenger of the Lord of Hosts.' But a most excellent messenger indeed of the Lord of Hosts he must be, who should bring forth those things, which were both so ambiguous to himself and so obscure to the people, that neither he should know what he himself said, nor they what they heard!

And what, throughout the Old Testament, in the 119th Psalm especially, is more frequently said in praise of the Scripture, than that it is itself a most certain and most clear light? For Ps. 119:105, celebrates its clearness thus: "Thy Word is a lamp unto my feet and a light unto my paths." He does not say only—thy Spirit is a lamp unto my feet; though he ascribes unto Him also His office, saying, "Thy good Spirit shall lead me into the land of uprightness." (Ps. 143:10) Thus the Scripture is called a "way" and a "path:" that is from its most perfect certainty.

NOW let us come to the New Testament. Paul says, (Rom. 1:2) that the Gospel was promised "by the Prophets in the Holy Scriptures." And, (Rom. 3:21) that the righteousness of faith was testified "by the Law and the Prophets." But what testimony is that, if it be obscure? Paul, however, throughout all his epistles makes the Gospel the Word of light, the Gospel of clearness; and he professedly and most copiously sets it forth as being so, 2 Cor. 3 and 4; where he treats most gloriously concerning the clearness both of Moses and of Christ.

Peter also says, (2 Pet. 1:19) "And we certainly have more surely the word of prophecy; unto which, ye do well that ye take heed, as unto a light shining in a dark place." Here Peter makes the Word of God a clear lamp, and all other things darkness: whereas, we make obscurity and darkness of the Word.

Christ also often calls Himself the "light of the world;" (John 8:12; 9:5) and John the Baptist, a "burning and a shining light," (John 5:35) certainly not on account of the holiness of his life, but on account of the Word which he ministered. In the same manner Paul calls the Philippians shining "lights of the world." (Phil. 2:15), because (says he,) ye "hold forth the word of life." (16) For life without the Word is uncertain and obscure.

And what is the design of the apostles in proving their preaching by the Scriptures? Is it that they may obscure their own darkness by still greater darkness? What was the intention of Christ, in teaching the Jews to "search the Scriptures" (John 5:39) as testifying of Him? Was it that He might render them doubtful concerning faith in Him? What was *their* intention, who having heard Paul, searched the Scriptures night and day, "to see if these things were so?" (Acts 17:11) Do not all these things prove that the Apostles, as well as Christ Himself, appealed to the Scriptures as the most clear testimonies of the truth of their discourses? With what boldness then do we make them 'obscure?'

Are these words of the Scripture, I pray you, obscure or ambiguous: "God created the heavens and the earth" (Gen. 1:1). "The Word was made flesh." (John 1:14) and all those other words which the whole world receives as articles of faith? Whence then, did they receive them? Was it not from the Scriptures? And what do those who at this day preach? Do they not expound and declare the Scriptures? But if the Scripture which they declare, be obscure, who shall assure us that their declaration is to be depended on? Shall it be guaranteed by another new declaration? But who shall make that declaration?—And so we may go on *ad infinitum*.

Briefly, if the Scripture be obscure or ambiguous, what need was there for its being sent down from heaven? Are we not obscure and ambiguous enough in ourselves, without an increase of it by obscurity, ambiguity, and darkness being sent down unto us from heaven? And if this be the case, what will become of that of the apostle, "All Scripture is given by inspiration of God, and is profitable for doctrine, for reproof, for correction?" (2 Tim. 3:16) Nay, Paul, you are altogether useless, and all those things which you ascribe unto the Scripture, are to be sought for out of the church fathers approved by a long course of ages, and from the Roman see! Wherefore, your sentiment must be revoked, where you write to Titus, (chap. 1:9) 'that a bishop ought to be powerful in doctrine, to exhort and to convince the gainsayers, and to stop the mouths of vain talkers, and deceivers of minds.' For how shall he be powerful, when you leave him the Scriptures in obscurity—that is, as weapons of flimsy rope and feeble straws, instead of a sword? And Christ must also, of necessity, revoke His word where He falsely promises us, saying, "I will give you a mouth and wisdom which all your adversaries shall not be able to resist," (Luke 21: 15) For how shall they not resist when we fight against them with obscurities and uncertainties? And why do you also, Erasmus, prescribe to us a form of Christianity, if the Scriptures be obscure to you!

But I fear I must already be burdensome, even to the insensible, by dwelling so long and spending so much strength upon a point so fully clear; but it was necessary, that that impudent and blasphemous saying, 'the Scriptures are obscure,' should thus be drowned. And you, too, my friend Erasmus, know very well what you are saying, when you deny that the Scripture is clear, for you at the same time drop into my ear this assertion: 'it of necessity follows therefore, that all your saints whom you cite, are much less clear.' And truly it would be so. For who shall assure us concerning their light, if you make the Scriptures obscure? Therefore they who deny the all-clearness and all-plainness of the Scriptures, leave us nothing else but darkness.

BUT here, perhaps, you will say—all that you have put forth is nothing to me. I do not say that the Scriptures are everywhere obscure (for who would be so mad?) but that they are obscure in this, and the like parts.—I answer: I do not advance these things against you only, but against all who are of the same sentiments with you. Moreover, I declare against you concerning the whole of the Scripture, that I will have no one part of it called obscure: and, to support me, stands that which I have brought forth out of Peter, that the Word of God is to us a "lamp shining in a dark place." (2 Peter 1:19) But if any part of this lamp do not shine, it is rather a part of the dark place than of the lamp itself. For Christ has not so illuminated us, as to wish that any part of His Word should remain obscure, even while He commands us to attend to it: for if it be not shiningly plain, His commanding us to attend to it is in vain.

Wherefore, if the doctrine concerning "Freewill" be obscure and ambiguous, it does not belong unto Christians and the Scriptures, and is, therefore to be left alone entirely, and classed among those "old wives' fables" (1 Tim. 4:7) which Paul condemns in contentious Christians. But if it does belong to Christians and the Scriptures, it ought to be clear, open, and manifest, and in every respect like unto all the other most evident articles of faith. For all the articles of faith which belong to Christians ought to be such, as may not only be most evident to themselves but so defended by manifest and clear Scriptures against the adversaries, as to stop the mouths of them all, that they shall not be able in anything to challenge. And this Christ has promised us, saying, "I will give you a mouth and wisdom which all your adversaries shall not be able to resist." But if our mouth be weak in this part, that the adversaries are able to resist, His saying, that no adversary shall be able to resist our mouth, is false. In the doctrine of "Freewill," therefore, we shall either have no adversaries, (which will be the case if it belong not unto us;) or, if it belong unto us, we shall have adversaries indeed, but such as will not be able to resist.

But concerning the inability of our adversaries to resist, (as that particular falls in here,) I would, by the way, observe that it is thus:—It does not mean, that they are forced to yield with the heart, or to confess, or be silent. For who can compel men against their will to yield, confess their error, and be silent? 'What (says Augustine), is more talkative than vanity?' But what is meant by their mouths being stopped, their not having a word to gainsay, and their saying many things, and yet, in the judgment of common sense, saying nothing, will be best illustrated by examples. *[Scripture examples omitted].* [56]

Luther marries Katherine von Bora

CHAPTER 3:

WHY THE WISE OF THIS WORLD

DO NOT UNDERSTAND THE GOSPEL

Luther demonstrates the Biblical truth that God's wisdom is unreachable by even the very best of human wisdom and that this is one more demonstration of the fact that man's will is in bondage to Satan.

48. BUT you ask—"if then the Scripture be quite clear, why have men of renowned talent, throughout so many ages, been blind upon this point?"—

I answer: they have been thus blind to the praise and glory of "Freewill;" in order that, that highly boasted-of 'power,' by which a man is 'able to apply himself unto those things that pertain unto eternal salvation,' might be eminently displayed; that very exalted power, which neither sees those things which it sees, nor hears those things which it hears, and much less, understands and seeks after them. For to this power, applies that which Christ and the evangelists so often bring forward out of Isaiah 6:9, "Hearing ye shall hear and shall not understand, and seeing ye shall see and shall not perceive." What is this besides saying, that "Freewill," or the human heart, is so bound by the power of Satan, that, unless it be made alive in a wonderful way by the Spirit of God, it cannot of itself see or hear those things which strike against the eyes and ears so manifestly, so real that one could reach out and touch them with the hand? So great is the misery and blindness of the human race! Thus also the Evangelists themselves, when they wondered how it could be that the Jews were not won over by the works and words of Christ, which were evidently incontrovertible and undeniable, satisfied themselves from that place of the Scripture, where it is shown, that man, left to himself, seeing seeth not, and hearing heareth not. And what can be more monstrous! "The light (says Christ) shineth in darkness, and the darkness comprehendeth it not." (John 1:5) Who could believe this? Who has heard the like—that the light should shine in darkness, and yet, the darkness still remain darkness, and not be enlightened!

Wherefore, it is no wonder in divine things, that throughout so many ages, men renowned for talent remained blind. It might have been a wonder in human things, but in divine things, it would rather have been a wonder if there had been one here and there that did not remain blind: that they all remained utterly blind alike, is no wonder at all. For what is the whole human race together, without the Spirit, but the kingdom of the devil (as I have said) and a confused chaos of darkness? And therefore it is, that Paul, (Eph 6:12) calls the devils, "the rulers of this darkness." And, (1 Cor. 2:8) he says, that none of the princes of this world knew the wisdom of God. What then must he think of the rest of the people, who asserts that the *princes* of this world are the slaves of darkness? For by princes, he means those greatest and highest ones, whom you call 'men renowned for talent.' And why were all the Arians blind? Were there not among them men renowned for talent? Why was Christ foolishness to the nations? Are there not among the nations men renowned for talent? "God (says Paul) knoweth the thoughts of the wise that they are vain." (1 Cor. 3:20) He chose not to say "of men," as the text to which he refers has it, but would point to the first and greatest among men, that from them we might form a judgment of the rest.—But upon these points more fully, perhaps, hereafter. Suffice it thus to have premised, in Exordium [1] , that the Scriptures are most clear, and that by them, our doctrines can be so defended that the adversaries cannot resist: but those doctrines that cannot be thus defended, are nothing to

---

[1]

Exordium is the heading of the sixth section of ten total sections in *The Bondage of the Will*. It would have preceded this comment. The word *exordium* is Latin, and means "A beginning or introductory part, especially of a speech or treatise." (www.thefreedictionary.com

us, for they belong not unto Christians. But if there be any who do not see this clearness, and are blind, or are outraged under the brilliant light of the sun, they, if they be wicked, manifest how great that dominion and power of Satan is over the sons of men, when they can neither hear nor comprehend the perfectly clear words of God, but are as one cheated by a juggler, who is made to think that the sun is a cold cinder, or to believe that a stone is gold. But if they fear God, they are to be numbered among those elect, who, to a certain degree, are led into error that the power of God may be manifest in us, without which, we can neither see nor do anything whatever. For the inability to comprehend the words of God, does not arise, as you pretend, from weakness of mind; nay, nothing is better adapted to the receiving of the words of God, than a weakness of the mind; for it was on account of

Martin Luther in prayer

these weak ones, and to these weak ones, that Christ came, and it is to them he sends His Word. But it is the wickedness of Satan enthroned and reigning in our weakness, and resisting the Word of God:—for if Satan did not do this, a whole world of men might be converted by one Word of God once heard, nor would there be need of more. [57]

CHAPTER 4:

ERASMUS' DEFINITION OF FREE WILL

AND LUTHER'S RESPONSE

> Luther demolishes Erasmus' definition of "freewill" by showing that
> it is internally contradictory because the definition of the term and
> the definition of the thing termed are against each other. Further,
> Erasmus' definition is illogical, unclear, evasive by introducing three
> kinds of "freewill", and based ultimately upon the idea that man is
> basically good, which is quite contrary to the Scriptures.

49. You [Erasmus] define "Freewill" thus,—

**"Moreover I consider Freewill in this light: that it is a power in the
human will, by which, a man may apply himself to those things which
lead unto eternal salvation, or turn away from the same."—**

**With a great deal of political ingenuity indeed, you have here stated
a mere simple definition, without declaring any *part* of it, (as all others
do); because, perhaps, you feared more shipwrecks than one. I therefore
am compelled to state the several parts myself. The thing defined by
itself, if it be closely examined, has a much wider extent than the
definition of it: and such a definition, the Sophists would call faulty:
that is, when the definition does not fully embrace the thing defined. For
I have shown before, that "Freewill" cannot be applied to anyone but
to God only. You may, perhaps, rightly assign to man some kind of will,
but to assign unto him "Freewill" in divine things, is going way too far.
For the term "Freewill," in the judgment of the ears of all, means, that
which can, and does do toward God, whatever it pleases, restrainable
by no law and no command. But you cannot call him *Free*, who is a
servant acting under the power of the Lord. How much less, then, can
we rightly call men or angels *free*, who so live under the sovereign
command of God, (to say nothing of sin and death,) that they cannot**

even continue their very existence for one moment by their own power.

Here then, at the outset, the definition of *the term*, and the definition of *the thing* termed, militate against each other: because the term signifies one thing, and the thing termed is, by experience, found to be another. It would indeed be more properly termed "Movable will," or "Changeable will."For in this way Augustine, and after him the Sophists, diminished the glory and force of the term, *free*; adding thereby this detriment, that they assign *changeable* to "Freewill." And it becomes us thus to speak, lest, by inflated and lofty terms of empty sound, we should deceive the hearts of men. And, as Augustine also thinks, we ought to speak according to a certain rule, in sober and proper words; for in teaching, simplicity and propriety of argumentation is required, and not highflown expressions of rhetorical persuasion. [58]

50. We come then to those parts of the definition, which are the hinge upon which the matter turns. Of these things some are manifest enough; the rest shun the light, as if conscious to themselves that they had every thing to fear: because, nothing ought to be expressed more clearly, and more decisively, than a definition; for to define obscurely, is the same thing as defining nothing at all.

The clear parts of the definition then are these:—'power of human will:' and 'by which a man can:' also, 'unto eternal salvation.' But these are *Andabatae [i.e. expressions which, like gladiators, will blindly take action]*:—'to apply:' and, 'to those things which lead:' also, 'to turn away.' What shall we divine that this 'to apply' means? And this 'to turn away,' also? And also what these words mean, 'which pertain unto eternal salvation?' Into what dark corner have these withdrawn their meaning? I seem as if I were engaged in dispute with a very Scotinian, or with Heraclitus himself, so as to be in the way of being worn out by a twofold labor. First, that I shall have to find out my adversary by groping and feeling about for him in pits and darkness, (which is an enterprise both daring and perilous,) and if I do not find him, to fight to no purpose with ghosts, and beat the air in the dark. And, secondly, if I should bring him out into the light, that then, I shall have to fight with him upon equal ground, when I am already worn out with hunting after him. I suppose, then, what you mean by the 'power of the human will' is this:—a power, or faculty, or disposition, or aptitude, to will or not to will, to choose or refuse, to approve or disapprove, and whatever other actions belong to the will. Now then, what it is for this same power 'to apply itself,' or 'to turn away,' I do not see: unless it be the very, willing or not willing, choosing or refusing, approving or disapproving; that is, the very action itself of the will. But may we suppose, that this power is a kind of medium, between the will itself and the action itself; such as, that by which the will itself charms forth the action itself of willing or not willing, or by which the action itself of willing or not willing is drawn forth? anything else beside this, it is impossible for one to imagine or think of. And if I am deceived, let the fault be my author's who has given the definition, not mine who examine it. For it is justly said among lawyers, 'his words who speaks obscurely, when he can speak more plainly, are to be interpreted against himself.' And here I wish to know nothing of our contemporaries and their subtleties, for we must come plainly to close quarters in what we say, for the sake of understanding and teaching.

And as to those words, 'which lead unto eternal salvation,' I suppose by them are meant the words and works of God, which are offered to the human will, that it might either apply itself to them, or turn away from them. But I call both the Law and the Gospel the words of God. By the Law, works are required; and by the Gospel, faith. For there are no other things which lead either unto the grace of God, or unto eternal salvation, but the word and the work of God: because grace or the spirit is the life itself, to which we are led by the word and the work of God.

BUT this life or salvation is an eternal matter, incomprehensible to the human capacity: as Paul shows, out of Isaiah, (1 Cor. 2:9) "Eye hath not seen nor ear heard, neither hath it entered into the heart of man to conceive the things which God hath prepared for them that love him." For when we speak of eternal life, we speak of that which is numbered among the chiefest articles of our faith. And what "Freewill" avails in this article Paul testifies, (1 Cor. 2:10). Also: "God (says he) hath revealed them unto us by His Spirit." As though he had said, the heart of no man will ever understand or think of any of those things, unless the Spirit shall reveal them; so far is it from possibility, that he should ever apply himself unto them or seek after them. Look at experience. What have the most exalted minds among the nations thought of a future life, and of the resurrection? Has it not been, that the more exalted they were in mind, the more ridiculous the resurrection and eternal life have appeared to them? Unless you mean to say, that those philosophers and Greeks at Athens, who, (Acts 17:18) called Paul, as he taught these things, a "babbler" and a "setter forth of strange gods," were not of exalted minds. Portius Festus, (Acts 26:24) calls out that Paul is "mad," on account of his preaching eternal life. What does Pliny bark forth in Book 7? What does Lucian also, that mighty genius? Were not they men who were greatly admired? Moreover to this day there are many, who, the more renowned they are for talent and extensive learning, the more they laugh at this article; and that openly, considering it a mere fable. And certainly, no man upon earth, unless imbued with the Holy Spirit, ever secretly knows, or believes in, or wishes for eternal salvation, no matter how much he may boast of it by his voice and by his pen. And may you and I, friend Erasmus, be free from this boasting leaven. So rare is a believing soul in this article!—Have I got the sense of this definition?

UPON the authority of Erasmus, then, *"Freewill," is a power of the human will, which can, of itself, will and not will to embrace the word and work of God, by which it is to be led to those things which are beyond its capacity and comprehension.* If then, it can will and not will, it can also love and hate. And if it can love and hate, it can, to a certain degree, do the Law and believe the Gospel. For it is impossible, if you can will and not will, that you should not be able by that will to begin some kind of work, even though, from the hindering of another, you should not be able to perfect it. And therefore, as among the works of God which lead to salvation, death, the cross, and all the evils of the world are numbered, human will can will its own death and perdition. Nay, it can will all things while it can will the embracing of the Word and work of God. For what is there that can be anywhere beneath, above, inside, and outside the Word and work of God, but God Himself? And what is there here left to grace and the Holy Spirit? This is plainly to ascribe deity to "Freewill." For to will to embrace the Law and the Gospel, not to will sin, and to will death, belongs to the power of God alone: as Paul testifies in more places than one. [59]

51. DO you see, friend Erasmus, that by this definition, you (though unwittingly I presume,) betray yourself, and make it manifest that you either know nothing of these things whatever, or that, without any consideration, and in a mere air of contempt, you write upon the subject, not knowing what you say nor whereof you affirm? And as I said before, you say less about, and attribute more to "Freewill," than all others put together; for you do not describe the whole of "Freewill," and yet you assign unto it all things. The opinion of the Sophists, or at least of the father of them, Peter Lombard, is far more tolerable: he says, '"Freewill" is the faculty of discerning, and then choosing also good, if with grace, but evil if grace be lacking.' He plainly agrees in sentiment with Augustine, that '"Freewill," of its own power, cannot do anything but fall, nor avail unto anything but to sin.' Wherefore Augustine also, Book 2, against Julian, calls "Freewill" 'under bondage,' rather than 'free.'—But you make the power of "Freewill" equal in both respects: that it can, by its own power, without grace, both apply itself unto good, and turn itself from evil. For you do not imagine

how much you assign unto it, by this pronoun *itself*, and *by itself*, when you say 'can apply itself:' for you utterly exclude the Holy Spirit with all His power, as a thing useless and unnecessary. Your definition, therefore, is condemnable even by the Sophists; who, were they not so blinded by hatred and fury against me, would be enraged at your book rather than at mine. But now, as your intent is to oppose Luther, all that you say is holy and catholic, even though you speak against both yourself and them,—so great is the patience of holy men!

Not that I say this, as approving the sentiments of the Sophists concerning "Freewill," but because I consider them more tolerable, for they approach nearer to the truth. For though they do not say, as I do, that "Freewill" is nothing at all, yet since they say that it can of itself do nothing without grace, they militate against Erasmus, nay, they seem to militate against themselves, and to be tossed to and fro in a mere quarrel of words, being more earnest for contention than for the truth, which is just as Sophists should be. But now, let us suppose that a Sophist of superior rank were brought before me, with whom I could speak upon these things apart, in familiar conversation, and should ask him for his liberal and candid judgment in this way:—'If anyone should tell you, that that was *free*, which of its own power could only go one way, that is, the bad way, and which could go the other way indeed, that is, the right way, but not by its own power, nay, only by the help of another—could you refrain from laughing in his face, my friend?'—For in this way, I will make it appear, that a stone, or a log of wood has "Freewill," because it can go upwards and downwards; although, by its own power, it can go only downwards, but can go upwards only by the help of another. And, as I said before, by meaning at the same time the thing itself, and also something else which may be joined with it or added to it, I will say, consistently with the use of all words and languages—all men are no man, and all things are nothing!

Thus, by a multiplicity of argumentation, they at last make "Freewill," free *by accident*; as being that, which may at some time be set free by another. But our point in dispute is concerning the thing itself, concerning the reality of "Freewill." If this be what is to be solved, there now remains nothing, let them say what they will, but the empty name of "Freewill."

The Sophists are deficient also in this—they assign to "Freewill," the power of discerning good from evil. Moreover, they treat as of no importance the doctrine of regeneration, and the renewing of the Spirit, and give that other *external aid*, as it were, to "Freewill:" but of this hereafter.—Let this be sufficient concerning the definition. Now let us look into the arguments that are to exalt this empty thing of a TERM. [60]

52. But I would briefly answer you here in your own words, 'The Scripture, in this place, is obscure and ambiguous;' therefore, it proves nothing to a certainty. But however, since I stand in the negative, I call upon you to produce that place which declares, in plain words, what "Freewill" is, and what it can do. And this perhaps you will do by about the time of the Greek Calends.—In order to avoid this necessity, you spend many fine sayings upon nothing; and moving along on the tip-toe of discreetness, cite numberless opinions concerning "Freewill," and make of Pelagius almost an Evangelist. Moreover, you fabricate a quadruple grace, so as to assign a sort of faith and charity even to the philosophers. And also that new fable, a triple law; of nature, of works, and of faith, so as to assert with all boldness, that the precepts of the philosophers agree with the precepts of the Gospel. Again, you apply that of Psalm 4:6. "The light of Thy countenance is settled upon us," which speaks of the knowledge of the very countenance of the Lord, that is, of faith, to blinded reason. If all of these things are taken into consideration by any Christian, they must compel him to suspect, that you are mocking and deriding the doctrines and religion of Christians: For to attribute these things as so much ignorance to him, who has illustrated all our doctrines with so much diligence, and stored them up in memory, appears to me very difficult indeed. [61]

53. How does that definition of "Freewill," let me ask you, which you gave us previously, square with this first opinion which you confess to be, 'very probable?' For you said that "Freewill" is a power of the human will, by which a man can apply himself unto good;' whereas here, you say and approve the saying, that 'man, without grace, cannot will good!' The definition, therefore, affirms what its example denies. And hence there are found in your "Freewill" both a YES and a NO:" so that, in one and the same doctrine and article, you approve and condemn us, and approve and condemn yourself. For do you think, that to 'apply itself to those things which pertain unto eternal salvation,' which power your definition assigns to "Freewill," is not to do good, when, if there were so much good in "Freewill," that it could apply itself unto good, it would have no need of grace? Therefore, the "Freewill" which you define is one, and the "Freewill" you defend is another. Hence then, Erasmus, outstripping all others, has two "Freewills;" and they, militating against each other!

BUT, setting aside that "Freewill" which the definition defines, let us consider that which the opinion proposes as contrary to it. You grant, that man, without special grace, cannot will good: (for we are not now discussing what the grace of God can do, but what man can do without grace) you grant, then, that "Freewill" cannot will good. This is nothing else but granting that it cannot 'apply itself to those things which pertain unto eternal salvation,' according to the tune of your definition. Nay, you say a little before, 'that the human will after sin, is so depraved, that having lost its liberty, it is compelled to serve sin, and cannot recall itself into a better state.' And if I am not mistaken, you make the Pelagians to be of this opinion. Now then I believe, my Proteus [2] has here no way of escape: he is caught and held fast in plain

---

2

Proteus: from Greek mythology. Proteus here represents a person who can change into whatever creature or object he wishes, thereby usually escaping capture and thereby escaping telling the truth. Luther calls Erasmus Proteus a number of times.

words:—' that the will, having lost its liberty, is tied and bound a slave to sin.' O noble Freewill! which, having lost its liberty, is declared by Erasmus himself, to be the slave of sin! When Luther asserted this, 'nothing was ever heard of so absurd;' 'nothing was more useless than that this paradox should be proclaimed abroad!' So much so, that even a Diatribe must be written against him! But perhaps no one will believe me, that these things are said by Erasmus. If the Diatribe be read in this part, it will be admired: but I do not so much admire it. For he who does not treat this as a serious subject, and is not interested in the cause, but is in mind alienated from it, and grows weary of it, cold in it, and disgusted with it, how shall not such an one everywhere speak absurdities, follies, and contrarieties, while, as one drunk or slumbering over the cause, he belches out in the midst of his snoring, It is so! it is not so! just as the different words sound against his ears? And therefore it is, that rhetoricians require a heartfelt involvement with the subject in the person discussing it. Much more then does theology require such a feeling, that it may make the person vigilant, sharp, intent, prudent, and determined.

If therefore "Freewill" without grace, when it has lost its liberty, is compelled to serve sin and cannot will good, I should be glad to know, what that desire is, what that endeavour is, which that first 'probable opinion' leaves it. It cannot be a good desire or a good endeavour, because it cannot will good, as the opinion affirms, and as you grant. Therefore, it is an evil desire and an evil endeavour that is left, which, when the liberty is lost, is compelled to serve sin.—But above all, what, I pray, is the meaning of this saying: 'this opinion leaves the desire and the endeavour, but does not leave what is to be ascribed to its own power.' Who can possibly conceive in his mind what this means? If the desire and the endeavour be left to the power of "Freewill," how are they not ascribed to the same? If they be not ascribed to it, how can they be left to it? Are then that desire and that endeavour before grace, left to grace itself that comes after, and not to "Freewill" so as to be at the same time left, and not left, to the same "Freewill?" If these things be not paradoxes, or rather enormities, then pray what are enormities?

BUT perhaps the Diatribe is dreaming this, that between these two, 'can will good' and 'cannot will good' there may be a middle ground; seeing that, *to will* is absolute, both in respect of good, and evil. So that thus, by a certain logical subtlety, we may steer clear of the rocks, and say, in the will of man there is a certain *willing*, which cannot indeed will good without grace, but which, nevertheless, being without grace, does not immediately will nothing but evil, but is a sort of *mere abstracted willing*, changeable, upwards unto good by grace, and downwards unto evil by sin. But then, what will become of that which you have said, that, 'when it has lost its liberty it is compelled to serve sin?' What will become of that desire and endeavour which are left? Where will be that power of 'applying itself to those things which pertain unto eternal salvation?' For that power of applying itself unto salvation, cannot be a mere *willing*, unless the salvation itself be said to be a nothing. Nor, again, can that desire and endeavour be a mere *willing*; for *desire* must strive and attempt something, (as good perhaps,) and cannot go forth into nothing, nor be absolutely inactive.

In a word, whichever way the Diatribe turns itself, it cannot keep clear of inconsistencies and contradictory assertions; nor avoid making that very "Freewill" which it defends, as much a bond-slave as it is a bond-slave itself. For, in attempting to liberate "Freewill," it is so entangled, that it is bound, together with "Freewill," in bonds indissoluble.

Moreover, it is a mere figment of the imagination that in man there is a middle ground, *a mere willing*, nor can they who assert this prove it; it arose from an *ignorance* of *things* and an *observance* of *terms*. As though the thing were always in reality, as it is set forth in terms; and there are with the Sophists many such misconceptions. Whereas the matter rather stands as Christ says, "He that is not with Me is against

Me." (Matt. 12:30) He does not say, He that is not with Me is yet not *against* Me, but *in the middle ground*. For if God be in us, Satan is from us, and it is present with us to will nothing but good. But if God be not in us, Satan is in us, and it is present with us to will evil only. Neither God nor Satan admit of a *mere abstracted willing* in us; but, as you yourself rightly said, when our liberty is lost we are compelled to serve sin: that is, we *will* sin and evil, we *speak* sin and evil, we *do* sin and evil.

Behold then! invincible and all-powerful truth has driven the witless Diatribe to that dilemma, and so turned its wisdom into foolishness, that whereas, its design was to speak against me, it is compelled to speak *for* me *against* itself; just in the same way as "Freewill" does anything good; for when it attempts so to *do*, the more it acts against evil the more it acts against good. So that the Diatribe is, in *saying*, exactly what "Freewill" is in *doing*. Though the whole Diatribe itself, is nothing else but a notable effort of "Freewill," condemning by defending, and defending by condemning: that is, being a twofold fool, while it would appear to be wise.

> This, then, is the state of the first opinion compared with itself:—it *denies that a man can will anything good; but yet that a desire remains; which desire, however, is not his own!*

> NOW let us compare this opinion with the remaining two.

> The next of these, is that opinion 'more severe still,' which holds, that "Freewill" avails unto nothing but to sin. And this indeed is Augustine's opinion, expressed, as well in many other places, as more especially, in his book "Concerning the Spirit and the Letter;" in (if I mistake not) the fourth or fifth chapter, where he uses those very words.

> The third, is that 'most severe' opinion; that "Freewill" is a mere empty term, and that every thing which we do, is done from necessity under the bondage of sin.—It is with these two that the Diatribe conflicts.

I here observe, that perhaps it may be, that I am not able to discuss this point intelligibly, from not being sufficiently acquainted with the Latin or with the German. But I call God to witness, that I wish nothing else to be said or to be understood by the words of the last two opinions than what is said in the first opinion: nor does Augustine wish anything else to be understood, nor do I understand anything else from his words, than that which the first opinion asserts: so that, the *three opinions* brought forward by the Diatribe are with me nothing else than my *one sentiment.* For when it is granted and established, that "Freewill," having once lost its liberty, is compulsively bound to the service of sin, and cannot will anything good: I, from these words, can understand nothing else than that "Freewill" is a mere empty term, whose reality is lost. And a lost liberty, according to my grammar, is no liberty at all. And to give the name of liberty to that which has no liberty, is to give it an empty term. If I am wrong here, let him set me right who can. If these observations be obscure or ambiguous, let him who can, illustrate and make them plain. I for my part, cannot call that health which is lost, health; and if I were to ascribe it to one who was sick, I should think I was giving him nothing else than an empty name. But away with these enormities of words. For who would bear such an abuse of the manner of speaking, as that we should say a man has "Freewill," and yet at the same time assert, that when that liberty is once lost, he is compulsively bound to the service of sin, and cannot will anything good? These things are contrary to common sense, and utterly destroy the common manner of speaking. The Diatribe is rather to be condemned, which in a drowsy way, foists forth its own words without any regard to the words of others. It does not, I say, consider what it is, nor how much it is to assert, that man, when his liberty is lost, is compelled to serve sin and cannot will anything good. For if it were at all vigilant or observant, it would plainly see, that the sentiment contained in the three opinions is one and the same, which it makes to be diverse and contrary.

For if a man, when he has lost his liberty, is compelled to serve sin, and cannot will good, what conclusion concerning him can be more justly drawn, than that he can do nothing but sin, and will evil?

And such a conclusion, the Sophists themselves would draw, even by *their* subtle reasoning. Wherefore, the Diatribe, unhappily, contends against the last two opinions, and approves the first; whereas, that is precisely the same as the other two; and thus again, as usual, it condemns itself and approves my sentiments, in one and the same article. [62]

Luther preaching peace to the army

CHAPTER 5

ON MAN'S COMPLETE INABILITY TO WILL GOOD

From the Scriptures and based upon common sense Luther shows that God gave commandments not as proof that man has the ability to choose good (as Erasmus and many others then and now argue), but to show man's absolute powerlessness to choose good.

54. But, what if I prove, that the nature of words and the use of speech even among men, are not always of that tendency, as to make a laughing stock of those to whom it is said, 'if thou wilt,' 'if thou shalt do it.' 'if thou shalt hear?'—How often do parents thus play with their children, when they bid them come to them, or do this or that, for this purpose only, that it may plainly appear to them how unable they are to do it, and that they may call for the aid of the parent's hand? How often does a faithful physician bid his obstinate patient do or omit those things which are either injurious to him or impossible, to the intent that, he may bring him, by an experience, to the knowledge of his disease or his weakness? And what is more general and common, than to use words of insult or provocation, when we would show either enemies or friends, what they can do and what they cannot do?

I merely go over these things, to show Reason her own conclusions, and how absurdly she tacks them to the Scriptures: moreover, how blind she must be not to see, that they do not always stand good even in human words and things. But the case is, if she see it to be done once, she rushes on headlong, taking it for granted, that it is done generally in all the things of God and men, thus making, according to the way of her wisdom, of a special case, a universal application.

If then God, as a Father, deal with us as with sons, that He might show us who are in ignorance our impotency, or as a faithful physician, that He might make our disease known unto us, or that He might insult His enemies who proudly resist His counsel; and for this end, say to us

by proposed laws (as being those means by which He accomplishes His design the most effectually) 'do,' 'hear,' 'keep,' or, 'if thou wilt,' 'if thou wilt do,' 'if thou wilt hear;' can this be drawn here from as a just conclusion—therefore, either we have free power to act, or God laughs at us? Why is this not rather drawn as a conclusion—therefore, God tries us, that by His Law He might bring us to a knowledge of our impotency, if we be His friends; or, He thereby righteously and deservedly insults and derides us, if we be His proud enemies.' For this, as Paul teaches, is the intent of the divine legislation. (Rom. 3:20; Gal. 3:19, 24) Because human nature is blind, so that it knows not its own powers, or rather its own diseases. Moreover, being proud, it self-conceitedly imagines, that it knows and can do all things. To remedy such pride and ignorance, God can use no means more effectual than His proposed Law: of which we shall say more in its place: let it suffice to have thus touched upon it here, to refute this conclusion of carnal and absurd wisdom:—'if thou wilt'—therefore you are able to will freely.

The Diatribe dreams that man is whole and sound as to human appearance, he is in his own affairs; and therefore, from these words, 'if thou wilt,' 'if thou wilt do,' 'if thou wilt hear,' it pertly argues, that man, if his will be not free, is laughed at. Whereas, the Scripture describes man as corrupt and a captive; and added to that, as proudly viewing with contempt, and ignorant of his corruption and captivity: and therefore, by those words, it goads him and rouses him up, that he might know, by a real experience, how unable he is to do any one of those things. [63]

55. For he *[Ecclesiasticus]* here speaks, not concerning the first man only, but concerning any man: though it is of little consequence whether you understand it concerning the first man, or any others. For although the first man was not impotent, from the assistance of grace, yet, by this

commandment, God plainly shows him how impotent he would be without grace. For if that man, who had the Spirit, could not by his new will, will good newly proposed, that is, obedience, because the Spirit did not add it unto him, what can we do without the Spirit toward the good that is lost! In this man, therefore, it is shown, by a terrible example for the breaking down of our pride, what our "Freewill" can do when it is left to itself, and not continually moved and increased by the Spirit of God. He could do nothing to increase the Spirit who had its firstfruits, but fell from the firstfruits of the Spirit. What then can we who are fallen, do towards the firstfruits of the Spirit which are taken away? Especially, since Satan, who cast Adam down by temptation alone, not then reigning in him, now reigns in us with full power! Nothing can be more forcibly brought against "Freewill," than this passage of Ecclesiasticus, considered together with the fall of Adam. But we have no room for these observations here. An opportunity may perhaps offer itself elsewhere.

> Meanwhile, it is sufficient to have shown, that Ecclesiasticus, in this place, says nothing whatever in favor of "Freewill" (which nevertheless they consider as their principal authority), and that these expressions and the like, 'if thou wilt,' 'if thou hear,' 'if thou do,' show, not what men *can do*, but what they *ought to do!*

ANOTHER passage is cited by our Diatribe out of Gen. 4:7, where the Lord says unto Cain, "Under thee shall be the desire of sin, and thou shalt rule over it."—"Here it is shown (says the Diatribe) that the motions of the mind toward evil can be overcome, and that they do not carry with them the necessity of sinning."—

These words, 'the motions of the mind toward evil can be overcome' though spoken with ambiguity, yet, from the scope of the sentiment, the consequence, and the circumstances, must mean this:—that "Freewill," has the power of overcoming its motions toward evil; and that, those motions do not bring upon it the necessity of sinning. Here, again; what is there excepted which is not ascribed unto "Freewill?" What need is there of the Spirit, what need of Christ, what need of God, if "Freewill" can overcome the motions of the mind toward evil! And where, again, is that 'probable opinion' which affirms, that "Freewill" cannot so much as will good? For here, the victory over evil is ascribed unto that, which neither wills nor wishes for good. The inconsiderateness of our Diatribe is really—too—too bad!

Take the truth of the matter in a few words. As I have before observed, by such passages as these, it is shown to man what he *ought to do*, not what he *can do*. It is said, therefore, unto Cain, that he ought to rule over his sin, and to hold its desires in subjection under him. But this he neither did nor could do, because he was already pressed down under the contrary dominion of Satan.—It is well known, that the Hebrews frequently use the *future indicative* [3] for the *imperative* [4]: as in Exod. 20:1-17. "Thou shalt have none other gods but Me," "Thou shalt not kill," "Thou shalt not commit adultery," and in numberless other instances of the same kind. Otherwise, if these sentences were taken indicatively, as they really stand, they would be *promises* of God; and as He cannot lie, it would come to pass that no man could sin; and then, as *commands*, they would be unnecessary; and if this were the case, then our interpreter would have translated this passage more correctly thus:—"let its desire be under thee, and rule thou over it," (Gen. 4:7) Even as it then ought also to be said concerning the woman, "Be thou under thy husband, and let him rule over thee," (Gen. 3:16) But that it was not spoken indicatively unto Cain is manifest from this:—it would then have been a *promise*. Whereas, it was not a promise; because, from

---

[3]

Future Indicative: By deduction, denoting a mood of verbs used chiefly to make statements regarding events in the future. (LCS)

[4]

Imperative: (Linguistics / Grammar) Grammar denoting a mood of verbs used in giving orders, making requests, etc. www.thefreedictionary.com

the conduct of Cain, the event proved the contrary.

THE third passage is from Moses, (Deut. 30:19) "I have set before thy face life and death, choose what is good . . ."—"What words (says the Diatribe) can be more plain? It leaves to man the liberty of choosing."—

I answer: What is more plain, than, that you are blind? How, I pray, does it leave the liberty of choosing? Is it by the expression 'choose'?—Therefore, as Moses says 'choose,' does it immediately come to pass that they do choose? Then, there is no need of the Spirit. And as you so often repeat and inculcate the same things, I shall be justified in repeating the same things also.—If there be a liberty of choosing, why has the 'probable opinion' said that "Freewill" cannot will good? Can it choose *not willing* or *against its will*? But let us listen to the illustration,

"It would be ridiculous to say to a man standing in a place where two ways met, You see two roads, go by whichever you will, when only one was open."

This, as I have before observed, is from the arguments of human reason, which thinks, that a man is mocked by a command impossible: whereas I say, that the man, by this means, is admonished and roused to see his own impotency.

True it is, that we are in a place where two ways meet, and that only one of them is open, yes, rather neither of them is open. But by the Law it is shown how impossible the one is, that is, to good, unless God freely give His Spirit; and how wide and easy the other is, if God leave us to ourselves. Therefore, it would not be said ridiculously, but with a necessary seriousness, to the man thus standing in a place where two ways meet, 'go by which thou wilt,' if he, being in reality impotent, wished to seem to himself strong, or contended that neither way was hedged up.

Wherefore, the words of the Law are spoken, not that they might assert the power of the will, but that they might illuminate the blindness of reason, that it might see that its own light is nothing, and that the power of the will is nothing. "By the Law (says Paul) is the knowledge of sin," (Rom. 3:20): he does not say—is the abolition of, or the escape from sin.

> The whole nature and design of the Law is to give knowledge only, and that of nothing else except of sin, but not to make known or communicate any power whatever. For knowledge is not power, nor does it communicate power, but it teaches and shows how great the impotency must there be, where there is no power. And what else can the knowledge of sin be, but the knowledge of our evil and infirmity?

For he does not say—by the Law comes the knowledge of strength or of good. The whole that the Law does, according to the testimony of Paul, is to make known sin.

And this is the place, where I take occasion to enforce this my general reply:—that man, by the words of the Law, is admonished and taught what *he ought to do*, not what *he can do*: that is, that he is brought to know his sin, but not to believe that he has any strength in himself. Wherefore, friend Erasmus, as often as you throw in my teeth the words of the Law, so often I throw in yours that of Paul, "By the Law is the knowledge of sin,"—not of the power of the will. Heap together, therefore, out of the large Concordances all the imperative words into one jumble, provided that, they be not words of the promise but of the requirement of the Law only, and I will immediately declare, that by them is always shown what men *ought to do*, not what they *can do*, or *do do*. And even common grammarians and every schoolboy in the street knows, that by verbs of the imperative mood, nothing else is signified than that which ought to be done, and that, what is done or can be done, is expressed by verbs of the indicative mood.

Thus, therefore, it comes to pass, that you theologians, are so senseless and so many degrees below even schoolboys, that when you have caught hold of one imperative verb you infer an indicative sense, as though what was commanded were immediately and even necessarily done, or possible to be done. [64]

56. Let me here then again make a distinction, between the words of the Scripture cited, and the conclusion of the Diatribe tacked to them. The words cited are imperative, and they say nothing but what ought to be done. For, Moses does not say, 'thou hast the power and strength to choose.' The words 'choose,' 'keep,' 'do,' convey the precept 'to keep,' but they do not describe the ability of man. But the conclusion tacked to them by that wisdom-aping Diatribe, infers thus:—therefore, man can do those things, otherwise the precepts are given in vain. To whom this reply must be made:—Madam Diatribe, you make a bad inference, and do not prove your conclusion, but the conclusion and the proof merely seem to be right to your blind, careless and inattentive self. But know, that these precepts are not given preposterously nor in vain; but that proud and blind mankind might, by them, learn the disease of his own impotency, if he should attempt to do what is commanded. [65]

57. The Diatribe is perpetually setting before us such a man, who either *can do* what is commanded, or at least *knows* that he *cannot do* it. Whereas, no such man is to be found. If there were such an one, then indeed, either impossibilities would be ridiculously commanded, or the Spirit of Christ would be in vain.

> The Scripture, however, sets forth such a man, who is not only bound, miserable, captive, sick, and dead, but who, by the operation of his lord, Satan, to his other miseries, adds that of blindness: so that he believes he is free, happy, at liberty, powerful, whole, and alive.

For Satan well knows that if men knew their own misery he could retain no one of them in his kingdom: because, it could not be, but that God would immediately pity and succour their known misery and calamity: seeing that He is with so much praise set forth, throughout the whole

Scripture as, being near unto the contrite in heart, that Isaiah 61:1-3, testifies, that Christ was sent "to preach the Gospel to the poor, and to heal the broken hearted."

Wherefore, the work of Satan is so to hold men, that they come not to know their misery, but that they presume that they can do all things which are enjoined. But the work of Moses the legislator is the contrary, even that by the Law he might make known to man his misery, in order that he might prepare him, thus bruised and confounded with the knowledge of himself, for grace, and might send him to Christ to be saved. Wherefore, the office of the Law is not ridiculous, but above all things serious and necessary. [66]

58. For it is well known, that even the schoolmen, except the Scotinians and our contemporaries, assert that man cannot love God with all his heart. Therefore, neither can he perform any one of the other precepts, for all the rest, according to the testimony of Christ, hang on this one. [Matt 22:40] [67]

Luther gives his defense at the Diet of Worms, April 1521

CHAPTER 6:

CONCERNING THE INSCRUTABLE WILL OF GOD

When comparing Scripture with Scripture, and with a knowledge of God's divine attributes, it is clear that God can actually have two different wills which sometimes seem in opposition, but which we know, by faith, are included in that knowledge which is not presently open to man. Thus, while God is seen as a Father not willing that any should perish, it is also clear that He does permit many to perish. In all of this God remains just.

59. BUT, *why it is*, that some are touched by the Law and some are not touched, why some receive the offered grace and some despise it, that is another question which is not here treated on by Ezekiel; because, he is speaking of THE PREACHED AND OFFERED MERCY OF GOD, not of that SECRET AND TO BE FEARED WILL OF GOD, who, according to His own counsel, ordains whom, and such as He will, to be receivers and partakers of the preached and offered mercy: which WILL, is not to be curiously inquired into, but to be adored with reverence as the most profound SECRET of the divine Majesty, which He reserves unto Himself and keeps hidden from us. [68]

60. God does many things which He does not make known unto us in His Word: He also wills many things which He does not in His Word make known unto us that He wills. Thus, He does not '*will* the death of a sinner,' that is, *in His Word*; but He *wills* it by that *will inscrutable*. But in the present case, we are to consider His Word only, and to leave that will inscrutable; seeing that, it is by His Word, and not by that will inscrutable, that we are to be guided: for who can direct himself according to a will inscrutable and incomprehensible? It is enough to know only, that there is in God a certain will inscrutable: but *what, why,*

---

and *how far* that will wills, it is not lawful to inquire, to wish to know, to be concerned about, or to reach unto—it is only to be feared and adored! Therefore it is rightly said, 'if God does not desire our death, it is to be laid to the charge of our own will, if we perish:' this, I say, is right, if you speak of GOD PREACHED. For He desires that all men should be saved, seeing that, He comes unto all by the Word of salvation, and it is the fault of the will which does not receive Him: as He says. (Matt. 23: 37) "How often would I have gathered thy children together, and thou wouldest not!" But WHY that Majesty does not take away or change this fault of the will IN ALL, seeing that, it is not in the power of man to do it; or why He lays that to the charge of the will, which the man cannot avoid, it becomes us not to inquire, and though you should inquire much, yet you will never find out: as Paul says, (Rom. 9:20) "Who art thou that repliest against God!" [69]

61. The God Incarnate, then, here speaks thus—"I WOULD and THOU WOULDST NOT!" The God Incarnate,—I say, was sent for this purpose—that He might desire, speak, do, suffer, and offer unto all, all things that are necessary unto salvation, although He should offend many, who, being either left or hardened by that secret will of Majesty, should not receive Him thus desiring, speaking, doing, and offering: as John 1:5, says, "The light shineth in darkness, and the darkness comprehended it not." And again, "He came unto His own, and His own received Him not." (11) It belongs also to this same God Incarnate, to weep, to lament, and to sigh over the perdition of the wicked, even while that will of Majesty, from purpose, leaves and reprobates some, that they might perish. Nor does it become us to inquire *why* He does so, but to revere that God who can do, and wills to do, such things.

Nor do I suppose that anyone will be so petty as to deny, that that will which here says, "How often would I!" was displayed to the Jews, even before God became Incarnate; seeing that they are accused of having slain the prophets, before Christ, and having thus resisted His will. For it is well known among Christians, that all things were done by the prophets in the name of Christ to come, who was promised that He should become Incarnate: so that, whatever has been offered unto men by the ministers of the word from the foundation of the world, may be rightly called, the Will of Christ.

BUT here Reason, who is always very knowing and verbose, will say,—This is an excellently invented evasion; that, as often as we are pressed close by the force of arguments, we might run back to that to-be-revered will of Majesty, and thus silence the disputant as soon as he becomes troublesome; just as astrologers do, who, by their invented epicycle, elude all questions concerning the motion of the whole heaven.—

I answer: It is no invention of mine, but a command supported by the Holy Scriptures. Paul, (Rom. 9:19) speaks thus: "Why therefore doth God find fault; for who hath resisted His will? Nay, but O man, who art thou that contenders with God?" "Hath not the potter power?" And so on. And before him, Isaiah 58:2, "Yet they seek Me daily, and desire to know My ways, as a nation that did righteousness: they ask of Me the ordinances of justice, and desire to approach unto God."

From these words it is, I think, sufficiently manifest that it is not lawful for men to search into that will of Majesty. And this subject is of that nature, that perverse men are here the most led to pry into that to-be-revered will, and therefore, there is here the greatest reason why they should be exhorted to silence and reverence. [70]

62. The New Testament, properly, consists of promises and exhortations, even as the Old, properly, consists of laws and threatenings. For in the New Testament, the Gospel is preached; which is nothing else than the Word, by which are offered unto us the Spirit, grace; and the remission of sins obtained for us by Christ crucified; and all entirely free, solely through the mercy of God the Father, thus

favoring us unworthy creatures, who deserve damnation rather than anything else.

And then follow exhortations, in order to animate those who are already justified, and who have obtained mercy, to be diligent in the fruits of the Spirit and of righteousness received, to exercise themselves in charity and good works, and to bear courageously the cross and all the other tribulations of this world. This is the whole sum of the New Testament. [71]

63. If you speak of the *consequence*, there is nothing either good or evil which has not its reward. And here arises an error, that, in speaking of merits and rewards, we agitate opinions and questions concerning *worthiness*, which has not existence, when we ought to be disputing concerning *consequences*. For there remains, as a necessary consequence the judgment of God and a hell for the wicked, even though they themselves neither conceive nor think of such a reward for their sins, nay, they utterly detest it; and, as Peter says, despise it. (2 Pet. 2:10-14.)

In the same manner, there remains a kingdom for the just, even though they themselves neither seek it nor think of it; seeing that it was prepared for them by their Father, not only before they themselves existed, but before the foundation of the world. Nay, if they should work good in order to obtain the Kingdom, they never would obtain it, but would be numbered rather with the wicked, who, with an evil and materialistic eye, seek the things of self even in God. Whereas, the sons of God, do good with a freewill, seeking no reward, but the glory and will of God only; ready to do good, even if (which is impossible) there were neither a Kingdom nor a hell. [72]

64. And the reason why it is declared in the Scriptures, that those things shall follow and take place after a good or bad life, is, that men might be instructed, admonished, awakened, and terrified. For as "by the Law is the knowledge of sin" (Rom. 3:20,) and an admonition of our impotency, and as from that, it cannot be inferred that we can do anything ourselves; so, by these promises and threats, there is conveyed an admonition, by which we are taught, what will follow sin and that impotency made known by the Law; but there is not, by them, anything of worthiness ascribed unto our merit. Wherefore, as the words of the Law are for instruction and illumination, to teach us what we ought to do, and also what we are not able to do; so the words of reward, while they signify what will be hereafter, are for exhortation and threatening, by which the just are animated, comforted, and raised up to go forward, to persevere, and to conquer; that they might not be wearied or disheartened either in doing good or in enduring evil; as Paul exhorts his Corinthians, saying, "Be ye steadfast, knowing that your labor is not in vain in the Lord." (1 Cor. 15: 58.) So also God supports Abraham, saying "I am thy exceeding great reward." (Gen. 15:1.) Just in the same manner as you would console anyone, by signifying to him, that his works certainly pleased God, which kind of consolation the Scripture frequently uses; nor is it a small consolation for anyone to know, that he so pleases God, that nothing but a good consequence can follow, even though it seem to him impossible.

TO this point pertain all those words which are spoken concerning the *hope* and *expectation*, that those things which we hope for will certainly come to pass. For the pious do not hope because of these words themselves, nor do they expect such things because they hope for them. So also the wicked by the words of threatening, and of a future judgment, are only terrified and cast down that they might cease and abstain from sin, and not become proud, secure, and hardened in their sins.

But if Reason should here turn up her nose and say—Why does God will these things to be done by His words, when by such words nothing is effected, and when the will can turn itself neither one way nor the

---

other? Why does He not do what He does apart from the Word, when He can do all things apart from the Word? For the will is of no more power, and does no more with the Word, if the Spirit to move within be lacking; nor is the will of less power, nor does it do less apart from the Word if the Spirit be present, seeing that all depends upon the power and operation of the Holy Spirit.

I answer: Thus it pleases God—not to give the Spirit apart from the Word, but through the Word; that He might have us as workers together with Him, while we sound forth in the Word apart from what He alone works by the breath of His Spirit within, wheresoever it pleases Him; which, nevertheless, He could do apart from the Word, but such is not His *will*. And who are we that we should inquire into the cause of the divine will? It is enough for us to know that such is the will of God; and it becomes us, bridling the rashness of reason, to reverence, love, and adore that will. For Christ, (Matt. 11:25-26) gives no other reason why the Gospel is hidden from the wise, and revealed unto babes, than this:—So it pleased the Father! In the same manner also, He can nourish us without bread; and indeed He has given a power which nourishes us without bread, as Matt. 4:4, says, "Man doth not live by bread alone, but by the Word of God:" but yet, it has pleased Him to nourish us by His Spirit within, by means of the Bread of Life, and quite apart from the bread baked in ovens. [73]

65. For God alone by His Spirit works in us both merit and reward, but He makes known and declares each, by His external Word, to the whole world; to the intent that, His power and glory and our impotency and vileness might be proclaimed even among the wicked, the unbelieving, and the ignorant, although those alone who fear God receive these things into their heart, and keep them faithfully; the rest despise them. [74]

66. AFTER this, it comes to Paul also, the most determined enemy to "Freewill," and even he is dragged in to confirm "Freewill;" "Or despisest thou the riches of His goodness, and patience, and long-suffering, not knowing that the goodness of God leadeth to repentance?"—(Rom. 2:4.)—"How (says the Diatribe) can the despising of the commandment be imputed where there is not a Freewill? How can God invite to repentance, who is the author of impenitence? How can the damnation be just, where the judge compels unto evil doing?"—

I answer: Let the Diatribe see to these questions itself. What are they unto us! The Diatribe said according to that 'probable opinion.' 'that "Freewill" cannot will good, and is of necessity compelled to serve sin.' How, therefore, can the despising of the commandment be charged on the will, if it cannot will good, and has no liberty, but is necessarily compelled to the service of sin? How can God invite to repentance who is the author of the reason why it cannot repent, while it leaves, or does not give grace to that, which cannot of itself will good? How can the damnation be just, where the judge, by taking away his aid, compels the wicked man to be left in his wickedness who cannot of his own power do otherwise?

All these conclusions therefore recoil back upon the head of the Diatribe. Or, if they prove any thing, as I said, they prove that "Freewill" can do all things: which, however, is denied by the Diatribe and by all. Thus these conclusions of reason torment the Diatribe, throughout all the passages of Scripture: seeing that, it must appear ridiculous and coldly useless, to enforce and exact with so much vehemence, when there is no one to be found who can perform: . . .

for the apostle's intent is, by means of these threats, to bring the impious and proud to a knowledge of themselves and of their impotency, that he might prepare them for grace when humbled by the knowledge of sin.

And what need is there to speak of, singly, all those parts which are brought forward out of Paul, seeing that, they are only a collection of imperative or conditional passages, or of those by which Paul exhorts Christians to the fruits of faith? Whereas the Diatribe, by its appended conclusions, forms to itself a power of "Freewill," such and so great, which can, without grace, do all things which Paul in his exhortations prescribes. Christians, however, are not led by "Freewill," but by the Spirit of God (Rom. 8:14): and to be led, is not to lead, but to be impelled, as a saw or an axe is impelled by a carpenter. [75]

Luther restrains and exhorts the peasants to obey the laws

CHAPTER 7:
ON BASIC RULES FOR INTERPRETING SCRIPTURE

The argument is made that Scripture must be interpreted by the plain rules of language and parts of speech, without introducing figures of speech or peripheral meanings of words.

67. THE Diatribe, having thus first cited numberless passages of Scripture, as it were a most formidable army in support of "Freewill," in order that it might inspire courage in the confessors and martyrs, the men saints and women saints on the side of "Freewill," and strike terror into all the fearful and trembling deniers of, and transgressors against "Freewill," imagines only a poor contemptible handful standing up to oppose "Freewill:" and therefore it brings forward no more than two Scriptures, which seem to be more prominent than the rest, to stand upon their side: intent only upon slaughter, and that, to be executed without much trouble. The one of these passages is from Exod. 9:13, "The Lord hardened the heart of Pharaoh:" the other is from Malachi 1:2-3, "Jacob have I loved, but Esau have I hated." Paul has fully explained both these passages in the Romans 9:11-17. But, according to the judgment of the Diatribe, what a detestable and useless discussion has he made of it! So that, did not the Holy Spirit know a little something of rhetoric, there would be some danger, lest, being broken at the outset by such an artfully managed show of contempt, He should despair of His cause, and openly yield to "Freewill" before the sound of the trumpet for the battle. But, however, I, as a recruit taken into the rear of those two passages, will display the forces on our side. Although, where the state of the battle is such, that one can put to flight ten thousand, there is no need of forces. If therefore, one passage shall defeat "Freewill," its numberless forces will profit it nothing.

IN this part of the discussion, then, the Diatribe has found out a new

way of eluding the most clear passages: that is, it will conceive that there is, in the most simple and clear passages, a *trope – [a literary device in which one thing is said, but something else is meant. A figure of speech, such as a metaphor]*. And as, before, when speaking in defense of "Freewill," it eluded all the imperative and conditional sentences of the Law by means of conclusions tacked on, and examples added to them; so now, where it designs to speak against us, it twists all the words of the divine promise and declaration whichever way it pleases, by means of a deceptive figure of speech which it has invented; thus, being everywhere an incomprehensible Proteus! Nay, it demands with a haughty brow, that this permission should be granted it, saying, that we ourselves, when pressed closely, are accustomed to escape by means of invented figures of speech: as in these instances:—"On which thou wilt, stretch forth thine hand:" (Ex. 8:5,) that is, grace shall extend your hand on whichever it will. "Make you a new heart:" (Ezek. 18:31,) that is, grace shall make you a new heart: and the like. It seems, therefore, an indignity offered, that Luther should be allowed to give forth an interpretation so forced and twisted, and that it should not be far more allowable to follow the interpretations of the most approved doctors of philosophy.

You see then, that here, the contention is not for the text itself, no, nor for conclusions and examples, but for deceptive figures of speech and interpretations. When then shall we ever have any plain and pure text, without deceptive figures of speech and conclusions, either for or against "Freewill?" Have the Scriptures no such texts anywhere? And shall the cause of "Freewill" remain forever in doubt, like a reed shaken with the wind, as being that which can be supported by no certain text, but which stands upon conclusions and figures of speech only, introduced by men mutually disagreeing with each other?

But let our sentiment rather be this:—that neither conclusion nor figure of speech is to be admitted into the Scriptures, unless the evident strife of the particulars, or the absurdity of any particular as militating against an article of faith, require it: but, that the simple, pure, and natural meaning of the words is to be adhered to, which is according to the rules of grammar, and to that common use of speech which God has given unto men. For if every one be allowed, according to his own lust, to invent conclusions and figures of speech in the Scriptures, what will the whole Scripture together be, but a reed shaken with the wind, or a kind of Vertumnus? Then, in truth, nothing could, to a certainty, be determined on or proved concerning any one article of faith, which you might not subject to raising trivial objections by means of some deceptive figure of speech. But every interpretation ought to be avoided as the most deadly poison, which is not absolutely required by the Scriptures itself.

See what happened to that figure-of-speech-inventor, Origen, in expounding the Scriptures. What just occasion did he give the malicious liar Periphery, to say, 'those who favor Origen, can be no great friends to Hieronymus.' What happened to the Arians by means of that deceptive figure of speech, according to which, they made Christ *God nominally*? What happened in our own times to those new prophets concerning the words of Christ, "This is my body?" One invented a figure of speech in the word "this," another in the word "is," another in the word "body. [5] " I have therefore observed this:—that all heresies and errors in the Scriptures, have not arisen from the simplicity of the words, as is the general report throughout the world, but from men not attending to the simplicity of the words, and hatching figures of speech and conclusions out of their own brain.

For example. "On whichever you will, stretch forth your hand." I, as far as I can remember, never put upon these words so violent an interpretation, as to say, 'grace shall extend your hand on whichever it

---

[5]

Luther here is referring to the doctrine of *transubstantiation* which the Roman Catholic Church developed between the years 1100 and 1200, approximately, according to www.wikipedia.com.

---

will:' "Make yourselves a new heart," 'that is, grace shall make you a new heart, and the like;' although the Diatribe maligns me thus in a public work, from being so carried away with, and tricked by its own deceptive figures of speech and conclusions, that it knows not what it says about anything. But I said this:—that by the words, 'stretch forth thine hand,' simply taken as they are, without false figures of speech or conclusions, nothing else is signified than what is required of us in the stretching forth of our hand, and what we ought to do; according to the nature of an imperative expression, with grammarians, and in the common use of speech.

But the Diatribe, not attending to this simplicity of the Word, but with violence producing conclusions and misleading figures of speech, interprets the words thus:—"Stretch forth thine hand;" that is, you are able by your own power to stretch forth your hand. "Make you a new heart," that is, you are able to make a new heart. 'Believe in Christ,' that is, you are able to believe in Christ. So that, with it, what is spoken imperatively, and what is spoken indicatively, is the same thing; or else, it is prepared to affirm that the Scripture is ridiculous and to no purpose. And these interpretations, which no grammarian will bear, must not be called, by Theologians, violent or invented, but the productions of the most approved doctors of philosophy received by so many ages.

But it is easy for the Diatribe to admit and follow figures of speech in this part of the discussion, seeing that it cares not at all whether what is said be certain or uncertain. Nay, it aims at making all things uncertain; for its design is that the doctrines concerning "Freewill" should be left alone, rather than searched into. Therefore, it is enough for it, to be enabled in any way to avoid those passages by which it finds itself closely pressed.

But as for me, who am maintaining a serious cause, and who am inquiring what is, to the greatest certainty, the truth, for the establishing of consciences, I must act very differently. For me, I say, it is not enough that you say there may be a figure of speech here: but I must inquire, whether there ought to be, or can be a figure of speech there. For if you cannot prove that there must, of necessity, be a figure of speech in that passage, you will effect nothing at all. There stands there this Word of God—"I will harden the heart of Pharaoh." (Ex. 4:21, Rom. 9:17-18) If you say that it can be understood or ought to be understood thus:—I will permit it to be hardened: I hear you say, indeed, that it may be so understood. And I hear this figure of speech used by everyone, 'I destroyed you, because I did not correct you immediately when you began to do wrong.' But here, there is no place for that interpretation. We are not here inquiring, whether that figure of speech be in use; we are not inquiring whether anyone can use it in that passage of Paul: but this is the point of inquiry—whether or not it be sure and safe to use this passage plainly as it stands, and whether Paul would have it so used. We are not inquiring into the use of an indifferent reader of this passage, but into the use of the author Paul himself.

What will you do with a conscience inquiring thus?—Behold God, as the Author, says, "I will harden the heart of Pharaoh:" the meaning of the word "harden" is plain and well known. But a man who reads this passage tells me, that in this place, 'to harden,' signifies 'to give an occasion of becoming hardened,' because, the sinner is not immediately corrected. But by what authority does he say this? With what design, by what necessity, is the natural signification of this passage thus twisted? And suppose the reader and interpreter should be in error, how shall it be proved that such a turn ought to be given to this passage? It is dangerous, nay, impious, thus to twist the Word of God, without necessity and without authority. Would you then comfort a poor soul thus laboring, in this way?—Origen thought so and so. Cease to search into such things, because they are peculiar and superficial. But he would answer you, this admonition should have been given to Moses or Paul before they wrote, and so also to God Himself, for it is they who vex us with these peculiar and superficial Scriptures.

THIS miserable imposter of figures of speech, therefore, profits the Diatribe nothing. But this Proteus of ours must here be held fast, and compelled to satisfy us fully concerning the figure of speech in this passage; and that, by Scriptures the most clear, or by miracles the most evident. For as to its mere opinion, even though supported by the labored industry of all ages, we give no credit to that whatever. But we urge on and press it home, that there can be here no figure of speech whatever, but that the Word of God is to be understood according to the plain meaning of the words. For it is not given unto us (as the Diatribe persuades itself to turn the words of God backwards and forwards according to our own lust: if that were the case, what is there in the whole Scripture, that might not be resolved into the philosophy of Anaxagoras—'that anything might be made from any thing?' And thus I will say, "God created the heavens and the earth:" that is, He stationed them, but did not make them out of nothing. Or, "He created the heavens and the earth;" that is, the angels and the devils; or the just and the wicked. Who, I ask, if this were the case, might not become a theologian at the first opening of a book?

Let this, therefore, be a fixed and settled point:—that since the Diatribe cannot prove that there is a figure of speech in these our passages which it utterly destroys, it is compelled to cede to us, that the words are to be understood according to their plain meaning; even though it should prove, that the same figure of speech is contained in all the other passages of Scripture, and used in common by every one. And by the gaining of this one point, all our arguments are at the same time defended, which the diatribe designed to refute; and thus, its refutation is found to effect nothing, to do nothing, and to be nothing. [76]

CHAPTER 8:
ON THE HARDENING OF PHARAOH'S AND OTHERS' HEARTS

The clear meaning of the Scriptures is that God did harden Pharaoh's heart as well as the hearts of others. No explanation which makes God passive in these events will fit the clear sense of the text of Scripture. This demonstrates that God's will is free while man's is not.

68. Whenever, therefore, this passage of Moses, "I will harden the heart of Pharaoh," is interpreted thus:—My long-suffering, by which I bear with the sinner, leads, indeed, others unto repentance, but it shall render Pharaoh more hardened in iniquity:—it is a pretty interpretation, but it is not proved that it ought to be so interpreted. But I am not content with what is said, I must have the proof.

And that also of Paul, "He hath mercy on whom He will have mercy, and whom He will He hardeneth, "(Rom. 9:18) is plausibly interpreted thus:—that is, God hardens when He does not immediately punish the sinner; and he has mercy when He immediately invites to repentance by afflictions.—But how is this interpretation proved?

And also that of Isaiah 63:17, "Why hast Thou made us to err from Thy ways and hardened our heart from Thy fear?" Be it so, that Jerome interprets it thus from Origen:—He is said to 'make to err' who does not immediately recall from error. But who shall assure us that Jerome and Origen interpret rightly? It is, therefore, a settled determination with me, not to argue upon the authority of any teacher whatever, but upon that of the Scripture alone. What Origens and Jeromes does the Diatribe, then, forgetting its own determination, set before us! especially when, among all the ecclesiastical writers, there are scarcely any who have handled the Holy Scriptures less to the purpose, and more absurdly, than Origen and Jerome. [77]

Only with a ridiculous exegetical license can Scripture be made to prove that man's will is capable of thwarting God's will, or that man's will is totally free of God's divinely ordained plan.

69. In a word: this liberty of interpretation, by a new and unheard-of kind of grammar, goes to confound all things. So that, when God says, "I will harden the heart of Pharaoh," you are to change the persons and understand it thus:—Pharaoh hardens himself by My long-suffering. God hardens our hearts;—that is, we harden ourselves by God's deferring the punishment. You, O Lord, have made us to err;—that is, we have made ourselves to err by Your not punishing us. So also, God's having mercy, no longer signifies His giving grace, or showing mercy, or forgiving sin, or justifying, or delivering from evil, but, on the contrary, signifies bringing on evil and punishing.

In fact, by these figures of speech matters will come to this:—you may say that God had mercy upon the children of Israel when He sent them into Assyria and to Babylon; because, He there punished the sinners, and there invited them, by afflictions, to repentance: and that, on the other hand, when He delivered them and brought them back, He did not then have mercy upon them, but hardened them; that is, by His longsuffering and mercy He gave them an occasion of becoming hardened. And also, God's sending the Saviour Christ into the world, will not be said to be the mercy, but the hardening of God; because, by this mercy, He gave men an occasion of hardening themselves. On the other hand, His destroying Jerusalem, and scattering the Jews even unto this day, is His having mercy on them; because, He punishes the sinners and invites them to repentance. Moreover, His carrying the

saints away into heaven at the day of judgment, will not be in mercy, but in hardening; because, by His long-suffering, He will give them an occasion of abusing it. But His thrusting the wicked down to hell, will be His mercy; because, He punishes the sinners.—Who, I pray you, ever heard of such examples of the mercy and wrath of God as these? [78]

Luther with Philipp Melanchthon

CHAPTER 10:
DID GOD REALLY SAY WHAT HE MEANT? ABSOLUTELY!

It is "carnal thoughtlessness" in man to trifle with the obvious and clear meaning of the Word of God in order to defend a false doctrine.

70. And be it so, that good men are made better both by the long-suffering and by the severity of God; yet, when we are speaking of the good and the bad loosely, these figures of speech, by an utter perversion of the common manner of speaking, will make, out of the mercy of God His wrath, and His wrath out of His mercy; seeing that, they call it the wrath of God when He does good, and His mercy when He afflicts.

Moreover, if God be said then to harden, when He does good and endures with long-suffering, and then to have mercy when He afflicts and punishes, why is He more particularly said to harden Pharaoh than to harden the children of Israel, or than the whole world? Did He not do good to the children of Israel? Does He not do good to the whole world? Does He not bear with the wicked? Does He not send rain upon the evil and upon the good? Why is He rather said to have mercy upon the children of Israel than upon Pharaoh? Did He not afflict the children of Israel in Egypt, and in the desert?—And be it so, that some abuse, and some rightly use, the goodness and the wrath of God; yet, according to your definition, to harden is the same as to indulge the wicked by long-suffering and goodness; and to have mercy is not to indulge, but to visit and punish. Therefore, with reference to God, He, by His continual goodness, does nothing but harden; and by His perpetual punishment, does nothing but show mercy.

BUT this is the most excellent statement of all—'that God is said to harden, when He indulges sinners by longsuffering; but to have mercy upon them, when He visits and afflicts, and thus, by severity, invites to

repentance.'

What, I ask, did God leave undone in afflicting, punishing, and calling Pharaoh to repentance? Are there not, in His dealings with him, ten plagues recorded? If, therefore, your definition stand good, that showing mercy is punishing and calling the sinner immediately, God certainly had mercy upon Pharaoh! Why then does not God say, I will have mercy upon Pharaoh? Whereas He says, "I will harden the heart of Pharaoh." For, in the very act of having mercy upon him, that is, (as you say) afflicting and punishing him, He says, "I will harden" him; that is, as you say, I will bear with him and do him good. What can be heard of more preposterous! Where are now your figures of speech? Where are your Origens? Where are your Jeromes? Where are all your most approved doctors of philosophy whom one poor creature, Luther, daringly contradicts?—But at this rate the flesh must unawares impel the man to confess who trifles with the words of God, and believes not their solemn importance! [79]

Younger Luther — 1827 portrait

CHAPTER 11:

SCRIPTURE'S FACTS AND ERASMUS' FIGURES

Luther continues to demolish Erasmus' careless figures of speech —
and to show that God's inscrutable will does overrule the will of man
according to God's divine plan.

71. The text of Moses itself, therefore, incontrovertibly proves, that here, these figures of speech are mere inventions and things of nought, and that by those words, "I will harden the heart of Pharaoh," something else is signified far different from, and of greater importance than, doing good, or affliction and punishment; because, we cannot deny, that both were tried upon Pharaoh with the greatest care and concern. For what wrath and punishment could be more unwavering and determined, than his being stricken by so many wonders and with so many plagues, that, as Moses himself testifies, the like had never been? Nay, even Pharaoh himself, repenting, was moved by them more than once; but he was not effectually moved, nor did he persevere in his temporary repentance. And what longsuffering or goodness of God could be greater, than His taking away the plagues so easily, hardening his sin so often, so often bringing back the good, and so often taking away the evil? Yet neither is of any avail. He still says, "I will harden the heart of Pharaoh!" You see, therefore, that even if *your* hardening and mercy, that is, your glosses and figures of speech, be granted to the greatest extent, as supported by use and by example, and as seen in the case of Pharaoh, there is yet a hardening that still remains; and that the hardening of which Moses speaks must, of necessity, be one thing, and that of which you dream, another.

BUT since I have to fight with fiction-framers and ghosts, let me turn to ghost-raising also. Let me suppose (which is an impossibility) that the figure of speech of which the Diatribe dreams avails in this

passage; in order that I may see which way the Diatribe will elude being compelled to declare that all things take place according to the will of God alone, and from necessity in us; and how it will clear God from being Himself the author and cause of our becoming hardened.—For if it be true that God is then said to "harden" when He bears with long-suffering, and does not immediately punish, these two positions still stand firm.

First, that man, nevertheless, *of necessity* serves sin. For when it is granted that "Freewill" cannot will anything good, (which kind of Freewill the Diatribe undertook to prove) then, by the goodness of a longsuffering God, it becomes nothing better, but of necessity worse.—Wherefore, it still remains that all that we do, is done *from necessity.* And next, that God appears to be just as cruel in this *bearing with us by His longsuffering*, as He does by being preached, as *willing to harden, by that will inscrutable.* For when He sees that "Freewill" cannot will good, but becomes worse by His enduring with longsuffering; by this very longsuffering He appears to be most cruel, and to delight in our miseries; seeing that He could remedy them if He willed, and might not thus endure with longsuffering if He willed, nay, that He could not thus endure unless He willed; for who can compel Him against His will? That will, therefore, without which nothing is done, being admitted, and it being admitted also, that "Freewill" cannot will anything good, all is advanced in vain that is advanced, either in excusation of God, or in accusation of "Freewill." For the language of "Freewill" is ever this:—I *cannot*, and God *will not.* What can I do! If He have mercy upon me by affliction, I shall be nothing benefited, but must of necessity become worse, unless He give me His Spirit. But this He gives me not, though He might give it me if He willed. It is certain, therefore, that He *wills not to give.*

NOR do the examples cited constitute anything to the purpose, where it is said by the Diatribe—"As under the same sun, mud is hardened and wax melted; as by the same shower, the cultivated earth brings forth fruit, and the uncultivated earth brings forth thorns; so, by the same long-suffering of God, some are hardened and some converted."—

For, we are not now dividing "Freewill" into two different natures, and making the one like mud, the other like wax; the one like cultivated earth, the other like uncultivated earth; but we are speaking concerning that one "Freewill" equally impotent in all men; which, as it cannot will good, is nothing but mud, nothing but uncultivated earth. Nor does Paul say that God, as the Potter, makes one vessel unto honour, and another unto dishonour, out of different kinds of clay, but He says, "Out of the same lump . . ." (Rom. 9:21) Therefore, as mud always becomes harder, and uncultivated earth always becomes more thorny; even so "Freewill," always becomes worse, both under the hardening sun of longsuffering, and under the softening shower of rain.

Luther requests permission to join the Augustinian monastery

If, therefore, "Freewill" be of one and the same nature and impotency in all men, no reason can be given why it should attain unto grace in one, and not in another; if nothing else be preached to all, but the goodness of a longsuffering, and the punishment of a mercy-showing God. For it is a granted position, that "Freewill" in all, is alike defined to be, 'that which cannot will good.' [80]

CHAPTER 12:

THE "WELL-MEANT OFFER" DOCTRINE [6]

AND GOD'S IMPOTENCE TO SAVE

How Erasmus' teaching will make God into the passive God envisioned by Aristotle.

72. And indeed, if it were not so, God could not elect anyone, nor would there be any place left for Election; but for "Freewill" only, as choosing or refusing the longsuffering and anger of God. And if God be thus robbed of His power and wisdom to elect, what will there be remaining but that idol Fortune, under the name of which, all things take place at random! Nay, we shall at length come to this: that men may be saved and damned without God's knowing anything at all about it; as not having determined by certain election who should be saved and who should be damned; but having set before all men in general His hardening goodness and longsuffering, and His mercy showing correction and punishment, and left them to choose for themselves whether they would be saved or damned; while He, in the mean time, should be gone, as Homer says, to an Ethiopian feast!

It is just such a God as this that Aristotle paints for us; that is, who sleeps Himself, and leaves every person to use or abuse God's

---

[6]

The term *"well-meant offer"* is understood to mean, within the context of its use, the concept that in the preaching of the gospel through all of Christ's servants down through the ages God has been making a "well meant offer" of salvation to all people, who being creatures of free will, can accept or reject the offer. Things are said such as "The Holy Spirit is a Gentleman and would never force Himself upon a person." This is the essence of Arminianism. Although Arminianism acknowledges the work of the Holy Spirit in salvation, and that salvation is by grace alone through faith alone, in practice it leaves the ultimate determination in *the will of the person* rather than in *the will of God.* Thus, a mere creature, may, in this scenario, defy God by rejecting the offer of salvation. This is to deny God's absolute sovereignty and omnipotence within His creation. The Scriptures nowhere support this doctrine. All of this author's experience as a believer confirms both the false doctrine within many congregations *and* the Biblical truths taught and defended here by Luther.

---

longsuffering and punishment just as he chooses. Nor can reason, of herself, form any other judgment than the Diatribe here does. For as she herself snores over, and looks with contempt upon divine things; she thinks concerning God, that He sleeps and snores over them too; not exercising His wisdom, will, and presence, in choosing, separating, and inspiring, but leaving the troublesome and irksome business of accepting or refusing His longsuffering and His anger, entirely to men. This is what we come to, when we attempt, by human reason, to limit and make excuses for God, not revering the secrets of His Majesty, but curiously prying into them—being lost in the glory of them, instead of making one excuse for God, we pour forth a thousand blasphemies! And forgetting ourselves, we blabber like madmen, both against God and against ourselves; when we are all the while supposing that we are, with a great deal of wisdom, speaking both for God and for ourselves.

Here then you see, what that figure of speech and gloss of the Diatribe, will make of God. And moreover, how excellently consistent the Diatribe is with itself; which before, by its one definition, made "Freewill" one and the same in all men: and now, in the course of its argumentation, forgetting its own definition, makes one "Freewill" to be cultivated and the other uncultivated, according to the difference of works, of good moral behavior, and of men: thus making two different "Freewills"; the one, that which cannot do good, the other, that which can do good, and that by its own powers before grace: whereas, its former definition declared that it could not, by those its own powers, will anything good whatever. Hence, therefore, it comes to pass that while we do not ascribe unto the will of God only, the will and power of hardening, showing mercy, and doing all things; we ascribe unto "Freewill" itself the power of doing all things without grace; which, nevertheless, we declared to be unable to do any good whatever without grace. The examples, therefore, of the sun and of the shower, do nothing at all to support the object under discussion. The Christian would use those examples more rightly, if he were to make the sun and the shower to represent the Gospel, as Psalm 19 does, and as does also Hebrews 6:7; and if he were to make the cultivated earth to represent the elect, and the uncultivated the reprobate; for the former are, by the Word, edified and made better, while the latter are offended and made worse. Or, if this distinction be not made, then, as to "Freewill" itself, that is in all men uncultivated earth and the kingdom of Satan. [81]

Luther in the vineyard with children

CHAPTER 13:
MORE REGARDING THE GOODNESS OF GOD
IN SPITE OF THE FACT THAT HE CHOOSES TO
LET SO MANY PERISH

God cannot be made to fit into man's concept of God. Man's reason
will never agree with God's way of thinking, or God's wisdom.

73. For it still remains absurd, (according to the judgment of reason,) that that God, who is just and good, should exact of "Freewill" impossibilities, and that, when "Freewill" cannot will good and of necessity serves sin, that sin should yet be laid to its charge and that, moreover, when He does not give the Spirit, He should, nevertheless, act so severely and unmercifully, as to harden, or permit to become hardened: these things, Reason will still say, are not becoming a God good and merciful. Thus, they too far exceed her capacity; nor can she so bring herself into subjection as to believe, and judge, that the God who does such things, is good; but setting aside faith, she wants to feel out and see, and comprehend *how* He can be good, and not cruel. But she will comprehend that, when this shall be said of God:—He hardens no one, He damns no one; but He has mercy upon all, He saves all; and He has so utterly destroyed hell, that no future punishment need be dreaded. It is thus that Reason blusters and contends, in attempting to clear God, and to defend Him as just and good.

But faith and the Spirit judge otherwise; who *believe* that God would be good, even though he should destroy all men. And to what profit is it, to weary ourselves with all these reasonings, in order that we might throw the fault of hardening upon "Freewill"! Let all the "Freewill" in the world, do all it can with all its powers, and yet, it never will give one proof, either that it can avoid being hardened where God gives not His Spirit, or merit mercy where it is left to its own powers. And what does

---

it signify whether it *be hardened*, or *deserve being hardened*, if the hardening be of necessity, as long as it remains in that impotency, in which, according to the testimony of the Diatribe, it cannot will good? Since, therefore, the absurdity is not taken out of the way by these figures of speech; or, if it be taken out of the way, greater absurdities still are introduced in their stead, and all things are ascribed unto "Freewill"; away with such useless and seducing figures of speech, and let us cleave close to the pure and simple Word of God! AS to the other point—'that those things which God has made, are very good: and that God did not say, for this purpose have I *made* thee, but "For this purpose have I *raised* thee *up*."'—

I observe, first of all, that this, Gen. 1, concerning the works of God being very good, was said before the fall of man. But it is recorded directly after, in Gen. 3 how man became evil,—when God departed from him and left him to himself. And from this one man thus corrupt, all the wicked were born, and Pharaoh also: as Paul says, "We were all by nature the children of wrath even as others." (Eph. 2:8). Therefore God *made* Pharaoh wicked; that is, from a wicked and corrupt seed: as He says in the Proverbs of Solomon, 16:4, "God hath made all things for Himself, yea, even the wicked for the day of evil:" that is, not by creating evil in them, but by forming them out of a corrupt seed, and ruling over them. This therefore is not a just conclusion—God made man wicked: therefore, he is not wicked. For how can he not be wicked from a wicked seed? As Ps. 51:5, says, "Behold I was conceived in sin." And Job 14: 4, "Who can make that clean which is conceived from unclean seed?" For although God did not make sin, yet, He ceases not to form and multiply that nature, which, from the Spirit being withdrawn, is defiled by sin. And as it is, when a carpenter makes statues of corrupt wood; so such as the nature is, such are the men made, when God creates and forms them out of that nature. Again: If you understand the words, "They were very good," as referring to the works of God after the fall, you will be pleased to observe, that this was said, not with reference to us, but with reference to God. For it is not said, "Man saw all the things that God had made, and behold they were very good." Many things seem very good unto God, and are very good, which seem unto us very evil, and are considered to be very evil. Thus, afflictions, evils, errors, hell, nay, all the very best works of God, are, in the sight of the world, very evil, and even damnable. What is better than Christ and the Gospel? But what is more execrated by the world? And therefore, how those things are good in the sight of God, which are evil in our sight, is known only unto God and unto those who see with the eyes of God; that is, who have the Spirit. But there is no need of argumentation so close as this, the preceding answer is sufficient. [82]

Luther burns papal bull — December 10, 1520

CHAPTER 14:

THE EFFECTS OF A SINFUL NATURE UPON THE SINNER

God gives to all men physical life, breath, and the motivation to act, but because man's nature is corrupt his acts are always evil in God's sight.

74. BUT here, perhaps, it will be asked, how can God be said to work evil in us, in the same way as He is said to harden us, to give us up to our own desires, to cause us to err, and so forth?

We ought, indeed, to be content with the *Word* of God, and simply to believe what that says; seeing that, the *works* of God are utterly unspeakable. But however, in compliance with Reason, that is, human foolery, I will just act the fool and the stupid fellow for once, and see by a little babbling, if I can produce any effect upon her.

First, then, both Reason and the Diatribe grant, that God works all in all; and that, without Him, nothing is either done or effective, because He is Omnipotent; and because, therefore, all things come under His Omnipotence, as Paul says to the Ephesians.

Now then, Satan and man being fallen and left to their own devices by God, cannot will good; that is, those things which please God, or which God wills; but are ever turned the way of their own desires, so that they cannot but seek their own. This, therefore, their will and nature, so turned from God, cannot be a nothing: nor are Satan and the wicked man a nothing: nor are the nature and the will which they have a nothing, although it be a nature corrupt and averse. That remnant of nature, therefore, in Satan and the wicked man, of which we speak, as being the creature and work of God, is not less subject to the divine omnipotence and action, than all the rest of the creatures and works of God.

Since, therefore, God moves and does all in all, He necessarily moves and does all in Satan and the wicked man. But He so does all in them, as they themselves are, and as He finds them: that is, as they are themselves averse and evil, being carried along by that motion of the Divine Omnipotence, they cannot but do what is averse and evil. Just as it is with a man driving a horse lame on one foot, or lame on two feet; he drives him just so as the horse himself is; that is, the horse moves badly. But what can the man do? He is driving along this kind of horse together with sound horses; one horse, indeed, goes badly, and the rest go well; but it cannot be otherwise, unless the horse be made healthy.

Here then you see that, when God works in and by evil men, the evils themselves are intrinsic, but yet, God cannot do evil, although He thus works the evils by evil men; because, being good Himself He cannot do evil; but He uses evil instruments, which cannot escape the sway and motion of His Omnipotence. The fault, therefore, is in the instruments, which God allows not to remain actionless; seeing that the evils are done as God Himself moves. Just in the same manner as a wood cutter would cut badly with a saw-edged or broken-edged axe. Hence it is, that the wicked man cannot but always err and sin; because, being carried along by the motion of the Divine Omnipotence, he is not permitted to remain motionless, but must will, desire, and act according to his nature. All this is a fixed certainty if we believe that God is Omnipotent!

It is, moreover, as certain that the wicked man is the creature of God; though being averse and left to himself without the Spirit of God, he cannot will or do good. For the Omnipotence of God requires that the wicked man cannot evade the motion and action of God, but, being of necessity subject to it, he yields; though his corruption and aversion to God, makes him such that he cannot be carried along and moved unto good. God cannot suspend His Omnipotence on account of his antipathy, nor can the wicked man change his antipathy. Wherefore it is, that he must continue of necessity to sin and err, until he be set right by the Spirit of God. Meanwhile, in all these, Satan goes on to reign in peace, and keeps his palace undisturbed under this motion of the Divine Omnipotence. [83]

75. BUT now follows the *act itself* of *hardening*, which is thus:—The wicked man (as we have said) like his prince Satan, is turned totally to the way of selfishness, and his own desires; he seeks not God, nor cares for the things of God; he seeks his own riches, his own glory, his own doings, his own wisdom, his own power, and, in a word, his own kingdom; and wills only to enjoy them in peace. And if anyone oppose him or wish to diminish any of these things, with the same aversion to God under which he seeks these, with the same aversion is he moved, enraged, and roused to indignation against his adversary. And he is as much unable to overcome this rage, as he is to overcome his desire of self-seeking; and he can no more avoid this seeking, than he can avoid his own existence; and this he cannot do, as being the creature of God, though a corrupt one.

The same is that fury of the world against the Gospel of God. For, by the Gospel, comes that "stronger than he," who overcomes the quiet possessor of the palace, and condemns those desires of glory, of riches, of wisdom, of self-righteousness, and of all things in which he trusts. This very irritation of the wicked, when God speaks and acts contrary to what they willed, is their hardening and their galling weight. For as they are in this state of aversion from the very corruption of nature, so they become more and more averse, and worse and worse, as this aversion is opposed or turned out of its way. And thus, when God threatened to take away from the wicked Pharaoh his power, he irritated and aggravated him, and hardened his heart the more, the more He came to him with His Word by Moses, making known His intention to take away his kingdom and to deliver His own people from his power: because He did not give him His Spirit within, but permitted his wicked corruption, under the dominion of Satan, to grow angry, to swell with pride, to burn with rage, and to go on still in a certain self-assured contempt.

LET no one think, therefore, that God, where He is said to *harden*, or to *work evil in us* (for to harden is to do evil), so does the evil as though He created evil in us anew, in the same way as a malignant liquor-seller, being himself bad, would pour poison into, or mix it up in, a container that was not bad, where the bottle itself did nothing but receive, or passively accomplish the purpose of the malignity of the poison-mixer. For when people hear it said by us, that God works in us both good and evil, and that we from mere necessity passively submit to the working of God, they seem to imagine, that a man who is good, or not evil himself, is *passive* while God *works* evil *in* him: not rightly considering that God, is far from being inactive in all His creatures, and never allows any one of them to enjoy a holiday from sinning.

But whoever wishes to understand these things let him think thus:—that God works evil in us, that is, by us, not from the fault of God, but from the fault of evil in us:—that is, as we are evil by nature, God, who is truly good, carrying us along by His own action, according to the nature of His Omnipotence, cannot do otherwise than do evil by us, as instruments, though He Himself be good; though by His wisdom, He overrules that evil will, to His own glory and to our salvation.

Thus God, *finding* the will of Satan evil, not *creating* it so, but leaving it while Satan sinningly commits the evil, carries it along by His working, and moves it which way He will; though that will ceases not to be evil by this motion of God.

In this same way also David spoke concerning Shimei. "Let him curse, for God hath bidden him to curse David." (2 Samuel 16:10). How could God bid to curse, an action so evil and virulent! There was nowhere an external precept to that effect. David, therefore, looks to this:—the Omnipotent God *says* and it is *done*: that is, He does all things by His external Word. Wherefore, here, the divine action and omnipotence, the good God Himself, carries along the will of Shimei, already evil together with all his members, and before incensed against David, and, while David is thus opportunely situated and deserving such blasphemy, commands the blasphemy, (that is, by his Word which is his act, that is, the motion of his action), by this evil and blaspheming instrument. [84]

76. IT is thus God hardens Pharaoh—He presents to his impious and evil will His Word and His work, which that will hates; that is, by its engendered and natural corruption. And thus, while God does not change by His Spirit that will within, but goes on presenting and enforcing; and while Pharaoh, considering his own resources, his riches and his power, trusts to them from the same naturally evil inclination; it comes to pass, that being inflated and uplifted by the imagination of his own greatness on the one hand, and swollen into a proud contempt of Moses coming in all humility with the simple and pure Word of God on the other, he becomes hardened; and then, the more and more irritated and chafed, the more Moses advances and threatens: whereas, this his evil will would not, of itself, have been moved or hardened at all. But as the omnipotent Agent moved it by that His inevitable motion, it must of necessity will one way or the other.—And thus, as soon as he presented to it outwardly, that which naturally irritated and offended it, then it was, that Pharaoh could not avoid becoming hardened; even as he could not avoid the action of the Divine Omnipotence, and the aversion or enmity of his own will.

Wherefore, the hardening of Pharaoh's heart by God, is wrought thus,:—God presents outwardly to his active hostility, that which he naturally hates; and then, He ceases not to move within, by His omnipotent motion, the evil will which He there finds. He, from the innate hostility of his will, cannot but hate that which is contrary to him, and trust to his own powers; and that, so obstinately, that he can neither hear nor feel, but is carried away in the possession of Satan like a madman or a person with a violent temper. [85]

CHAPTER 15: LET GOD BE GOD!

> God hardened Pharaoh's heart; He permitted Adam to fall through disobedience. God has done and will do many things for which there are no simple or easy answers. It is not for man to judge God or His works, but for man to adore the Almighty.

77. If I have brought these things home with convincing persuasion, the victory in this point is mine. And having exploded the figures of speech and glosses of men, I understand the words of God simply; so that there is no necessity for clearing God or accusing Him of iniquity. For when He says, "I will harden the heart of Pharaoh," He speaks simply: as though He should say, I will so work, that the heart of Pharaoh shall be hardened: or, by My operation and working, the heart of Pharaoh shall be hardened. And how this was to be done, we have heard:—that is, by My general motion, I will so move his very evil will, that he shall go on in his course and lust of willing, nor will I cease to move it, nor can I do otherwise. I will, nevertheless, present to him My word and work; against which, that evil impelling force will run; for he, being evil, cannot but will evil while I move him by the power of My Omnipotence.

Thus God with the greatest certainty knew, and with the greatest certainty declared, that Pharaoh would be hardened; because, He with the greatest certainty knew that the will of Pharaoh could neither resist the motion of His Omnipotence nor put away its own natural hostility, nor receive its adversary Moses; and that, as that evil will still remained, he must, of necessity, become worse, more hardened, and more proud, while, by his course and evil impelling force, trusting to his own powers, he ran against that which he would not receive, and which he despised.

Here therefore, you see, it is confirmed even by this very Scripture, that "Freewill" can do nothing but evil while God, who is not deceived from ignorance nor lies from iniquity, so surely promises the hardening of Pharaoh; because, He was certain, that an evil will could will nothing but evil, and that, as the good which it hated was presented to it, it could

not but become worse and worse.

IT then remains, that someone may ask—Why then does not God cease from that motion of His Omnipotence, by which the will of the wicked is moved to go on in evil, and to become worse? I answer: this is to wish that God, for the sake of the wicked, would cease to be God; for this you really desire, when you desire His power and action to cease; that is, that He should cease to be good, lest the wicked should become worse.

Again, it may be asked—Why does He not then change, in His motion, those evil wills which He moves? This belongs to those secrets of Majesty, where "His judgments are past finding out." Nor is it ours to search into, but to adore these mysteries. If "flesh and blood" here take offense and murmur, let it murmur, but it will be just where it was before. God is not, on that account, changed! And if numbers of the wicked be offended and "go away," yet, the elect shall remain! The same answer will be given to those who ask—Why did He permit Adam to fall? And why did He make all of us to be infected with the same sin, when He might have kept him, and might have created us from some other seed, or might first have cleansed that, before He created us from it?—

> God is that Being, for whose will no cause or reason is to be assigned, as a rule or standard by which it acts; seeing that, nothing is superior or equal to it, but it is itself the rule of all things. For if it acted by any rule or standard, or from any cause or reason, it would be no longer the *will of* GOD. Wherefore, what God wills, is not therefore right, because He ought or ever was bound so to will; but on the contrary, what takes place is therefore right, because He so wills. A cause and reason are assigned for the will of the creature, but not for the will of the Creator; unless you set up, over Him, another Creator. [86]

78. But (to say nothing about that, which I have already proved from the Scriptures, that Pharaoh cannot rightly be said to be hardened, 'because, being borne with by the long-suffering of God, he was not

immediately punished,' seeing that, he was punished by so many plagues;) if *hardening* be 'bearing with divine longsuffering and not immediately punishing;'what need was there that God should so many times promise that He would then harden the heart of Pharaoh when the signs should be wrought, who now, before those signs were wrought, and before that hardening, was such, that, being inflated with his success, prosperity and wealth, and being borne with by the divine long-suffering and not punished, inflicted so many evils on the children of Israel? You see, therefore, that this figure of speech of yours does not speak to the purpose in this passage; seeing that it applies generally unto *all*, as sinning *because* they are borne with by the divine longsuffering. And thus, we shall be compelled to say that all are hardened, seeing that, there is no one who does not sin; and that no one [1] sins but he who is borne with by the divine longsuffering. Wherefore, this hardening of Pharaoh is another hardening, independent of that general hardening as produced by the longsuffering of the divine goodness.

THE more immediate design of Moses then is, to announce, not so much the hardening of Pharaoh, as the veracity and mercy of God; that is, that the children of Israel might not distrust the promise of God, wherein He promised that He would deliver them. (Ex. 6:1). And since this was a matter of the greatest consequence, He foretells them the difficulty, that they might not fall away from their faith; knowing that all those things which were foretold must be accomplished in the order in which, He who had made the promise had arranged them. As if He had said, "I will deliver you, indeed, but you will with difficulty believe it; because Pharaoh will so resist and put off the deliverance. Nevertheless, I exhort you to believe; for the whole of his putting off

---

[1] I.e. The apparent inference is that people only have a lifetime to sin because God, in great longsuffering, foregoes the immediate death sentence upon sin, giving people time to repent, rather than killing them instantly so that they could sin no more.

shall, by My way of operation, only be the means of My working the more and greater miracles to your confirmation in faith, and to the display of My power; that henceforth, you might the more steadily believe Me upon all other occasions."

In the same way does Christ also act, when, at the last supper, He promises His disciples a kingdom. He foretells them numberless difficulties, such as, His own death and their many tribulations; to the intent that, when it should come to pass, they might afterwards the more steadily believe.

And Moses by no means obscurely sets forth this meaning, where he says, "But Pharaoh shall not send you away, that many wonders might be wrought in Egypt." And again, "For this purpose have I raised thee up, that I might show in thee My power; that My name might be declared throughout all the earth." (Ex. 9:16; Rom. 9:17). Here, you see that Pharaoh was for this purpose hardened, that he might resist God and put off the redemption; in order that, there might be an occasion given for the working of signs, and for the display of the power of God, that He might be declared and believed on throughout all the earth. And what is this but showing, that all these things were said and done to confirm faith, and to comfort the weak, that they might afterwards freely believe in God as true, faithful, powerful, and merciful? Just as though He had spoken to them in the kindest manner, as to little children, and had said, "Be not terrified at the hardness of Pharaoh, for I work that very hardness Myself; and I, who deliver you, have it in My own hand. I will only use it, that I may thereby work many signs, and declare My Majesty, for the furtherance of your faith."

And this is the reason why Moses generally after each plague repeats, "And the heart of Pharaoh was hardened, so that he would not let the people go; as the Lord had spoken." (Ex. 7:13, 22; 8:15, 32; 9:12, etc.). What is the intent of this, "as the Lord had spoken," but, that the Lord might appear true, who had foretold that he should be hardened?—Now, if there had been any *vertibility [that is, any ability to change the mind in response to God's command]* or *liberty* of *will* in Pharaoh, which could turn either way, God could not with such certainty have foretold his hardening. But as He promised, who could neither be deceived nor lie, it of certainty and of necessity came to pass, that he was hardened: which could not have taken place, had not the hardening been totally apart from the power of man, and in the power of God alone, in the same manner as I said before; namely, from God being certain, that He should not omit the general operation of His Omnipotence in Pharaoh, or on Pharaoh's account; nay, that He could not omit it.

Moreover, God was equally certain that the will of Pharaoh; being naturally evil and averse, could not consent to the Word and work of God, which was contrary to it, and that therefore, while the evil impelling force of willing was preserved in Pharaoh by the Omnipotence of God, and while the hated Word and work *[of God]* was continually set before his eyes perceptibly, nothing else could take place in Pharaoh but offense and the hardening of his heart. For if God had then omitted the action of His Omnipotence in Pharaoh, when He set before him the word of Moses which he hated, and the will of Pharaoh might be supposed to have acted alone by its own power, then, perhaps, there might have been room for a discussion, which way it had power to turn. But now, since it was led on and carried away by its own willing, no violence was done to its will, because it was not forced against its will, but was carried along, by the natural operation of God, to will naturally just as it was by nature, that is, evil; and therefore, it could not but run against the Word, and thus become hardened. Hence we see, that this passage makes most forcibly against "Freewill"; and in this way—God who promised could not lie, and if He could not lie, then Pharaoh could not but be hardened. [87]

CHAPTER 16:
REGARDING JUDAS THE TRAITOR
AND GOD'S DIVINE FOREKNOWLEDGE

This is a prime example of God's foreknowledge necessitating man's choices.

79. If God foreknew that Judas would be a traitor, Judas became a traitor of necessity; nor was it in the power of Judas nor of any other creature to alter it, or to change that will; though he did what he did willingly, not by compulsion; for that *willing* of his was his *own* work; which God, by the motion of His Omnipotence, moved on into action, as He does everything else.—God does not lie, nor is He deceived. This is a truth evident and invincible. There are no obscure or ambiguous words here, even though all the most learned men of all ages should be so blinded as to think and say to the contrary. No matter how much, therefore, you may turn your back upon it, yet, the convicted conscience of yourself and all men is compelled to confess, that, IF GOD BE NOT DECEIVED IN THAT WHICH HE FOREKNOWS, THAT WHICH HE FOREKNOWS MUST, OF NECESSITY, TAKE PLACE. If it were not so, who could believe His promises, who would fear His threatenings, if what He promised or threatened did not of necessity take place! Or, how could He promise or threaten, if His foreknowledge could be deceived or hindered by our mutability – *[that is, by any innate ability of ours to change our minds in obedience or disobedience to God]*! This all-clear light of certain truth manifestly stops the mouths of all, puts an end to all questions, and forever settles the victory over all evasive subtleties. We know, indeed, that the foreknowledge of man is fallible.

We know that an eclipse does not therefore take place, because it is foreknown; but, that it is therefore foreknown, because it is to take

place. But what have we to do with this foreknowledge? We are disputing about the foreknowledge of God! And if you do not ascribe to this, the necessity of the consequent foreknown, you take away faith and the fear of God, you destroy the force of all the divine promises and threatenings, and thus deny deity itself. [88]

Luther translating the Bible into German

CHAPTER 17:
GOD'S FOREKNOWLEDGE IMPOSES NECESSITY UPON OUR WILLS

> If God foreknows a thing, it necessarily happens. The Potter does as He wills with the clay. The clay has no will or say in what happens to it.

80. For what was inquired into by that question concerning the will of God? Was it not this—whether or not it imposed a necessity on our will? Paul, then, answers that it is thus:—"He will have mercy on whom He will have mercy, and whom He will He hardeneth. It is not of him that willeth, nor of him that runneth, but of God that showeth mercy." (Rom. 9:15-16,18). Moreover, not content with this explanation, he introduces those who murmur against this explanation in their defense of "Freewill," and affirm that there is no merit allowed, that we are damned when the fault is not our own, and the like, and stops their murmuring and indignation: saying, "Thou wilt say then, Why doth He yet find fault? for who hath resisted His will?" (Rom. 9:19).

Do you not see that this is addressed to those, who, hearing that the will of God imposes necessity on us, say, "Why doth He yet find fault?" That is, Why does God thus insist, thus urge, thus exact, thus find fault? Why does He accuse, why does He reprove, as though we men could do what He requires if we would? He has no just cause for thus finding fault; let Him rather accuse His own will; let Him find fault with that; let Him press His requirement upon that; "For who hath resisted His will?" Who can obtain mercy if He wills not? Who can become softened if He wills to harden? It is not in our power to change His will, much less to resist it, where He wills us to be hardened; by that will, therefore, we are compelled to be hardened, whether we will or no.

If Paul had not explained this question, and had not stated to a certainty, that necessity is imposed on us by the foreknowledge of God, what need was there for his introducing the murmurers and complainers saying that His will cannot be resisted? For who would have murmured or been indignant, if he had not found necessity to be stated? Paul's words are not ambiguous where he speaks of resisting the will of God. Is there anything ambiguous in what resisting is, or what His will is? Is it at all ambiguous concerning what he is speaking, when he speaks concerning the will of God? Let the myriads of the most approved doctors of philosophy be blind; let them pretend, if they will, that the Scriptures are not quite clear, and that they tremble at a difficult question; we have words the most clear which plainly speak thus: "He will have mercy on whom He will have mercy, and whom He will He hardeneth:" and also, "Thou wilt say to me then, Why doth He yet complain, for who hath resisted His will?"

The question, therefore, is not difficult; nay, nothing can be more plain to common sense, than that this conclusion is certain, stable, and true:—if it be pre-established from the Scriptures, that God neither errs nor is deceived; then, whatever God *foreknows*, must, of *necessity*, take place.

It would be a difficult question indeed, nay, an impossibility, I confess, if you should attempt to establish both the *foreknowledge* of God and the *"Freewill"* of man. For what could be more difficult, nay a greater impossibility, than to attempt to prove that contradictions do not clash; or that a number may, at the same time, be both nine and ten?

There is no difficulty on our side of the question, but it is sought for and introduced, just as ambiguity and obscurity are sought for and violently introduced into the Scriptures.

The apostle, therefore, restrains the impious who are offended at these most clear words, by letting them know, that the divine will is accomplished, by necessity in us; and by letting them know also, that it is defined to a certainty, that they have nothing of liberty or "Freewill"left, but that all things depend upon the will of God alone. But he restrains them in this way:—by commanding them to be silent, and to revere the majesty of the divine power and will, over which we have no control, but which has over us a full control to do whatever it will. And yet it does us no injury, seeing that it is not indebted to us, it never received anything from us, it never promised us anything but what itself pleased and willed.

THIS, therefore, is not the place; this is not the time for adoring those Corycian[2] caverns, but for adoring the true Majesty in its to-be-feared, wonderful, and incomprehensible judgments; and saying, "Thy will be done in earth as it is in heaven." (Matt. 6:10). Whereas, we are nowhere more irreverent and rash, than in trespassing and arguing upon these very inscrutable mysteries and judgments. And while we are pretending to a great reverence in searching the Holy Scriptures, those which God has commanded to be searched, we search not; but those which He has forbidden us to search into, those we search into and none other; and that with an unceasing foolhardiness, not to say, blasphemy.

> For is it not searching with recklessness, when we attempt to make the all-free foreknowledge of God to harmonize with our freedom, prepared to take foreknowledge from God, rather than lose our own liberty? Is it not utter stupidity, when He imposes necessity upon us, to say, with murmurings and blasphemies, "Why doth He yet find fault? for who hath resisted His will?" (Rom. 9:19). Where is the God by nature most merciful? Where is He who "willeth not the death of a sinner?" Has He then created us for this purpose only, that He might delight Himself in the torments of men? And many things of the same kind, which will be howled forth by the damned in hell to all eternity. [89]

---

[2]**Corycian Cavern:** The reference is to some famous very large, dark caverns on the slopes of Mount Parnassus in Greece, named after the nymph Corycia.

81. But however, natural Reason herself is compelled to confess, that the living and true God must be such an one as, by His own liberty, to impose necessity on us. For He must be a ridiculous God, or idol rather, who did not, to a certainty, foreknow the future, or was liable to be deceived in events, when even the Gentiles ascribed to their gods 'fate inevitable." And He would be equally ridiculous, if He could not do, and did not all things, or if anything could be done without Him. If then the foreknowledge and omnipotence of God be granted, it naturally follows, as an indisputable consequence that we neither were made by ourselves, nor live by ourselves, nor do anything by ourselves, but by His Omnipotence. And since He at the first foreknew that we should be such, and since He has made us such, and moves and rules over us as such, how, I ask, can it be pretended, that there is any liberty in us to do, in any respect, otherwise than He at first foreknew and now proceeds in action!

Wherefore, the foreknowledge and Omnipotence of God, are diametrically opposite to our "Freewill." And it must be, that either God is deceived in His foreknowledge and errs in His action, (which is impossible) or we act, and are acted upon, according to His foreknowledge and action.

But by the Omnipotence of God, I mean, not that power by which He *does not* many things that He *could do*, but that *actual power* by which He powerfully *works all in all*, in which sense the Scripture calls Him Omnipotent.

This Omnipotence and foreknowledge of God, I say, utterly abolishes the doctrine of "Freewill."

No pretext can here be framed about the obscurity of the Scripture, or the difficulty of the subject-point: the words are most clear, and known to every school-boy; and the point is plain and easy and stands proven

by judgment of common sense; so that the series of ages, of times, or of persons, either writing or teaching to the contrary, be it as great as it may, amounts to nothing at all.

BUT it is this, that seems to give the greatest offense to common sense or natural reason,—that the God, who is set forth as being so full of mercy and goodness, should, of His mere will, leave men, harden them, and damn them, as though He delighted in the sins, and in the great and eternal torments of the miserable. To think thus of God, seems iniquitous, cruel, intolerable; and it is this that has given offense to so many and great men of so many ages.

And who would not be offended? I myself have been offended more than once, even unto the deepest abyss of despair; nay, so far, as even to wish that I had never been born a man; that is, before I was brought to know how healthful that despair was, and how near it was unto grace. Here it is, that there has been so much toiling and laboring, to excuse the goodness of God, and to accuse the will of man. Here it is, that distinctions have been invented between the *ordinary* will of God and the *absolute* will of God: between the necessity of the consequence, and the necessity of the thing consequent: and many other inventions of the same kind. By which, nothing has ever been effected but an imposition upon the unlearned, by vanities of words, and by "oppositions of science falsely so called." (1 Tim 6:20) For after all, a conscious conviction has been left deeply rooted in the heart both of the learned and the unlearned, if ever they have come to an experience of these things; and a knowledge, that our necessity is a consequence that must follow upon the belief of the foreknowledge and Omnipotence of God.

And even natural Reason herself, who is so offended at this necessity, and who invents so many contrivances to take it out of the way, is compelled to grant it upon her own conviction from her own judgment, even though there were no Scripture at all. For all men find these sentiments written in their hearts, and they acknowledge and approve them (though against their will) whenever they hear them treated on.—First, that God is Omnipotent, not only in power but in action (as I said before): and that, if it were not so, He would be a ridiculous God.—And next, that He knows and foreknows all things, and neither can err nor be deceived. These two points then being granted by the hearts and minds of all, they are at once compelled, from an inevitable consequence, to admit,—that we are not made from our own will, but from necessity: and moreover, that we do not what we will according to the contrived law of "Freewill," but as God foreknew and proceeds in action, according to His infallible and immutable counsel and power. Wherefore, it is found written alike in the hearts of all men, that there is no such thing as "Freewill"; though that writing be obscured by so many contending disputations, and by the great authority of so many men who have, through so many ages, taught otherwise. Even as every other law also, which, according to the testimony of Paul, is written in our hearts, is then acknowledged when it is rightly set forth, and then obscured, when it is confused by wicked teachers, and drawn aside by other opinions. [90]

82. I NOW return to Paul. If he does not, Rom. 9, explain this point, nor clearly state our necessity from the foreknowledge and will of God; what need was there for him to introduce the example of the "potter," who, of the "same lump" of clay, makes "one vessel unto honour and another unto dishonour?" (Rom. 9:21). What need was there for him to observe, that the thing formed does not say to him that formed it, "Why hast thou made me thus?" (20). He is there speaking of men; and he compares them to clay, and God to a potter. This example, therefore, stands coldly useless, nay, is introduced ridiculously and in vain, if it be not his sentiment, that we have no liberty whatever. Nay, the whole of the argument of Paul, wherein he defends grace, is in vain. For the design of the whole epistle is to show, that we can do nothing, even when

we seem to do well; as he in the same epistle testifies, where he says, that Israel which followed after righteousness, did not attain unto righteousness; but that the Gentiles which followed not after it did attain unto it. (Rom. 9: 30-31). Concerning which I shall speak more at large hereafter, when I produce my forces.

The fact is, the Diatribe designedly keeps back the body of Paul's argument and its scope, and comfortably satisfies itself with prating upon a few detached and corrupted terms. Nor does the exhortation which Paul afterwards gives, Rom. 11, at all help the Diatribe; where he says, "Thou standest by faith, be not high-minded;" (20), again, "and they also, if they shall believe, shall be grafted in,. . . (23);" for he says nothing there about the ability of man, but brings forth imperative and conditional expressions; and what effect they are intended to produce, has been fully shown already. Moreover, Paul, there anticipating the boasters of "Freewill," does not say, they *can* believe, but he says, "God is able to graft them in again." (23). To be brief: The Diatribe moves along with so much hesitation, and so lingeringly, in handling these passages of Paul, that its conscience seems to give the lie to all that it writes. For just at the point where it ought to have gone on to the proof, it for the most part, stops short with a 'But of this enough;' 'But I shall not now proceed with this;' 'But this is not my present purpose;' 'But here they should have said so and so;' and many evasions of the same kind; and it leaves off the subject just in the middle; so that, you are left in uncertainty whether it wished to be understood as speaking on "Freewill," or whether it was only evading the sense of Paul by means of vanities of words. And all this is being just in its character, as not having a serious thought upon the cause in which it is engaged. But as for me I dare not be thus cold, thus always on the tip-toe of political correctness, or thus move to and fro as a reed shaken with the wind. I must assert with certainty, with constancy, and with ardour; and prove what I assert solidly, appropriately, and fully. [91]

Because of God's foreknowledge it was impossible that Judas could have changed his mind about betraying Jesus. Judas betrayed Christ willingly.

83. Have I not said in all my books again and again, that my dispute, on this subject, is about *the necessity of immutability*? I know that the Father begets willingly, and that Judas willingly betrayed Christ. But I say, this willing, in the person of Judas, was decreed to take place from immutability and certainty, if God foreknew it. Or, if men do not yet understand what I mean,—I make two necessities: the one a *necessity of force*, in reference to *the act*; the other a *necessity of immutability* in reference to *the time*. Let him, therefore, who wishes to hear what I have to say, understand, that I here speak of the *latter*, not of the *former*: that is, I do not dispute whether Judas became a traitor willingly or unwillingly, but whether or not it was decreed to come to pass, that Judas *should will* to betray Christ *at a certain time* infallibly predetermined of God!

But only listen to what the Diatribe says upon this point—"With reference to the immutable foreknowledge of God, Judas was of necessity to become a traitor; nevertheless, Judas had it in his power to change his own will."—

Do you understand, friend Diatribe, what you say? (To say nothing of that which has been already proved, that the will cannot will anything but evil.) How could Judas change his own will, if the immutable foreknowledge of God stand granted! Could he change the foreknowledge of God and render it fallible!

Here the Diatribe gives it up, and, leaving its standard, and throwing down its arms, runs from its post, and hands over the discussion to the subtleties of the schools concerning the necessity of the consequence and of the thing consequent: pretending—'that it does not wish to engage in the discussion of points so nice.' [92]

84. What is it to me if "Freewill" be not compelled, but do what it does willingly? It is enough for me that you grant that it is of necessity, that it does willingly what it does; and that, it cannot do otherwise if God foreknew it would be so. If God foreknew either that Judas would be a traitor, or that he would change his willing to be a traitor, then whichsoever of the two God foreknew, must, of necessity, take place, or God will be deceived in His foreknowledge and prediction, which is impossible. This is the effect of the necessity of the consequence, that is, if God foreknows a thing, that thing must of necessity take place; that is, there is no such thing as "Freewill." This necessity of the consequence, therefore, is not 'obscure or ambiguous;' so that, even if the most learned men of all ages were blinded, yet they must admit it, because it is so manifest and plain, as to be actually palpable _[i.e. actually quite discernable to the natural human senses]._ [93]

Luther ministering to the sick

CHAPTER 19: JACOB AND ESAU

The destinies of both men, both in physical and spiritual blessings, were foreknown by God and therefore came to pass of necessity. More on the foolishness of trying to force God into a box formed from our own ungodly reasoning. It is as unjust to reward the undeserving (as God does by taking his chosen ones to heaven) as it is to punish those who (in our ungodly judgment) are undeserving, whom God sends to hell.

85. Now let us proceed to the remaining part concerning *Jacob and Esau*, who are spoken of as being "not yet born." (Rom. 9:11). . . . And if it be allowed that this passage, Gen. 25:21-23 is to be understood in a temporal sense (which is not the true sense) yet it is rightly and effectually cited by Paul, when he proves from it, that it was not of the "merits" of Jacob and Esau, "but of Him that calleth," that it was said unto Rebecca, "the elder shall serve the younger." (Rom.9:11-16).

Paul is argumentatively considering, whether or not they attained unto that which was said of them, by the power or merits of "Freewill"; and he proves that they did not; but that Jacob attained unto that unto which Esau attained not, solely by the grace "of Him that calleth." And he proves that by the incontrovertible words of the Scripture: that is, that they were "not yet born:" and also, that they had "done neither good nor evil." This proof contains the weighty sum of his whole subject point, and by the same proof our subject point is settled also.

The Diatribe, however, having dissemblingly passed over all these particulars, with an excellent rhetorical stratagem, does not here argue at all upon merit, (which, nevertheless, it undertook to do, and which this subject point of Paul requires), but quibbles about temporal bondage, as though that were at all to the purpose;—but it is merely that it might not seem to be overthrown by the all-forcible words of

Paul. For what had it, which it could yelp against Paul in support of "Freewill"?

What did "Freewill" do *for* Jacob, or what did it do *against* Esau, when it was already determined, by the foreknowledge and predestination of God, before either of them was born, what should be the portion of each; that is, that the one should serve and the other rule? Thus the rewards were decreed before the workmen wrought or were born. It is to this that the Diatribe ought to have answered. Paul contends for this:—that neither had done either good or evil, and yet, that by the divine sentence the one was decreed to be servant, the other lord. The question here is not whether that servitude pertained unto salvation, but from what *merit* it was imposed on him who had not deserved it. But it is wearisome to contend with these depraved attempts to pervert and evade the Scripture.

BUT however, that Moses does not intend their servitude only, and that Paul is perfectly right, in understanding it concerning eternal salvation, is manifest from the text itself. And although this is somewhat outside of our present purpose, yet I will not allow Paul to be contaminated with the calumnies of the sacrilegious. The oracle in Moses is thus—"Two manner of people shall be separated from thy bowels, and the one people shall be stronger than the other people; and the elder shall serve the younger." (Gen. 25:23).

Here, manifestly, are two people distinctly mentioned. The one, though the younger, is received into the grace of God; to the intent that, he might overcome the other; not by his own strength, indeed, but by a favoring God; for how could the younger overcome the elder unless God were with him!

Since, therefore, the younger was to be the people of God, it is not only the external rule or servitude which is there spoken of but all that pertains to the Spirit of God; that is, the blessing, the Word, the Spirit, the promise of Christ, and the everlasting kingdom. And this the Scripture more fully confirms afterwards, where it describes Jacob as being blessed, and receiving the promises and the kingdom.

All this Paul briefly intimates, where he says, "The elder shall serve the younger:" and he sends us to Moses, who treats upon the particulars more fully.... AND with respect to that of Malachi which Paul annexes, "Jacob have I loved, but Esau have I hated;" (Mal. 1:2-3) the Diatribe perverts by a threefold contrivance. The first is – "If (it says) you stick to the letter, God does not love as we love, nor does He hate anyone: because, passions of this kind do not pertain unto God."—

What do I hear! Are we now inquiring *whether or not* God loves and hates, and not rather *why* He loves and hates? Our inquiry is, from what merit it is in us that He loves or hates. We know well enough, that God does not love or hate as we do; because, we love and hate mutably, but He loves and hates from an eternal and immutable nature; and hence it is, that accidents and passions do not pertain unto Him.

And it is this very state of the truth, that of necessity proves "Freewill" to be nothing at all; seeing that, the love and hatred of God towards men is immutable and eternal; existing, not only before there was any merit or work of "Freewill," but before the worlds were made; and that all things take place in us from necessity, accordingly as He loved or hated from all eternity. So that, not the love of God only, but even the *manner* of His love imposes on us necessity. . . . Hence, therefore, what God wills, that He loves and hates. Now then, tell me, for what merit did God love Jacob or hate Esau, before they wrought, or were born? Wherefore it stands manifest, that Paul most rightly quotes Malachi in support of the passage from Moses: that is, that God therefore called Jacob before he was born, because He loved him; but that He was not first loved by Jacob, nor moved to love him from any merit in him. So that, in the cases of Jacob and Esau, it is shown—what ability there is in our "Freewill"! . . . Paul proves out of Malachi, that affliction was laid on Esau without any desert, by the hatred of God only: and this he does, that he might thus conclude, that there is no such thing as "Freewill." . . . How then will your assertion stand good, that the prophet is here speaking of temporal affliction, when he testifies, in the plainest words, that he is speaking of the two people as proceeding from the two patriarchs, the one received to be a people and saved, and the other left and at last destroyed? To be received as a people, and not to be received as a people, does not pertain to temporal good and evil only, but unto all things. For our God is not the God of temporal things only, but of all things. Nor does God will to be your God so as to be worshipped with one shoulder, or with a lame foot, but with all your might, and with all your heart, that He may be your God as well here, as hereafter, in all things, times, and works. . . . Our point in dispute is, *by what merit* or *work* they attain unto that faith by which they are grafted in, or unto that unbelief by which they are cut off. This is the point that belongs to you as the teacher of "Freewill." And pray, describe to me this merit.

> Paul teaches us that this comes to them by no work of their own, but only according to the love or the hatred of God: and when it is come to them, he exhorts them to persevere, that they be not cut off. But this exhortation does not prove what we *can do*, but what we *ought to do* . . . .

When Paul, 2 Tim. 2:20, had said, that "in a great house there are vessels of gold and silver, wood and earth, some to honour and some to dishonour," he immediately adds, "If a man therefore purge himself from these, he shall be a vessel unto honour . . ." (21) Paul does not say, if anyone shall purify himself from his own filth, but "from these;" that is, from the vessels unto dishonour: so that the sense is, if anyone shall remain separate, and shall not mingle himself with wicked teachers, he shall be a vessel unto honour. . . . So that, from all the circumstances of the words and mind of Paul, you may understand that he is establishing the doctrine concerning the diversity and use of vessels.

The sense, therefore, is this:—seeing that so many depart from the faith, there is no comfort for us but the being certain that "the foundation of God standeth sure, having this seal, The Lord knoweth them that are His. And let every one that calleth upon the name of the Lord depart from evil." (2 Tim. 2:19). This then is the cause and efficacy of the example—that God knows His own! Then follows the example—that there are different vessels, some to honour and some to dishonour. By this it is proved at once that the vessels do not prepare themselves, but that the Master prepares them. And this is what Paul means, where he says, "Hath not the potter power over the clay, etcetera." (Rom. 9:21). Thus, the example of Paul stands most effective: and that to prove, that there is no such thing as "Freewill" in the sight of God.

After this, follows the exhortation: "If a man purify himself from these,". . . and for what purpose this is, may be clearly collected from what we have said already. It does not follow from this, that the man can purify himself. Nay, if anything be proved hereby it is this:—that "Freewill" can purify itself without grace. For he does not say, if grace purify a man; but, "if a man purify himself." But concerning imperative and conditional passages, we have said enough. Moreover, the example is not set forth in conditional, but in indicative verbs —that the elect and the reprobate are as vessels of honour and of dishonour. In a word, if this stratagem stands good, the whole argument of Paul comes to nothing. For in vain does he introduce vessels murmuring against God as the potter if the fault plainly appears to be in the vessel, and not in the potter. For who would murmur at hearing him damned, who *merited* damnation!

THE other absurd objection the Diatribe gathers from Madam Reason; who is called Human Reason—that the fault is not to be laid on the vessel, but on the potter: especially, since He is such a potter, who *creates* the clay as well as *molds* it.—"Whereas, (says the Diatribe) here the vessel is cast into eternal fire, which merited nothing: except that it had no power of its own."

In no single place does the Diatribe more openly betray itself than in this. For it is here heard to say, in other words indeed, but in the same meaning, that which Paul makes the impious to say, "Why doth He yet complain? for who hath resisted His will?" (Rom. 9:19). This is that which Reason cannot receive and cannot bear. This is that which has offended so many men renowned for talent, who have been received through so many ages. Here they require, that God should act according to human laws, and do what seems right unto men, or cease to be God! 'His secrets of Majesty, say they, do not better His character in our estimation. Let Him render a reason why He is God, or why He wills and does that which has no appearance of justice in it. It is as if one should ask a cobbler or a collar-maker to take the seat of judgment.'

Thus, an unregenerated person does not think God worthy of so great glory, that it should believe Him to be just and good, while He says and does those things which are above that which the volume of Justin and the fifth book of Aristotle's Ethics have defined to be justice. That Majesty which is the Creating Cause of all things must bow to one of the dregs of His creation: and that Corycian cavern must, *vice versa*, fear its spectators. It is absurd that He should condemn him who cannot avoid the merit of damnation. And, on account of this absurdity, it must be false, that "God has mercy on whom He will have mercy, and hardens whom He will." (Rom. 9:18). He must be brought to order. He must have certain laws prescribed to Him, that he damn not anyone but him, who, according to our judgment, deserves to be damned.

And thus, an effectual answer is given to Paul and his example. He must recall it, and allow it to be utterly ineffective: and must so modify and mold it, that this potter (according to the Diatribe's interpretation) make the vessel to dishonour from *merit preceding*; in the same manner in which He rejected some Jews on account of unbelief, and received Gentiles on account of faith. But if God works thus, and has respect unto merit, why do those impious ones murmur and expostulate? Why do they say, "Why doth He find fault? for who hath resisted His will?" (Rom. 9:19). And what need was there for Paul to restrain them? For who wonders even, much less is indignant and expostulates, when anyone is damned who merited damnation? Moreover where remains the power of the potter to make whatever vessel He will, if, being subject to merit and laws, He is not permitted to make what He *will*, but is required to make what He *ought*? The respect of merit militates against the power and liberty of making what He will: as is proved by that "good man of the house," who, when the workmen murmured and expostulated concerning their right, objected in answer, "Is it not lawful for me to do what I will with mine own?"—These are the arguments, which will not permit the gloss of the Diatribe to be of any avail.

BUT let us, I pray you, suppose that God *ought to be* such an one, who should have respect unto *merit* in those who are to be *damned*. Must we not, in like manner; also require and grant, that He ought to have respect unto merit in those who are to be *saved*?

For if we are to follow Reason, it is equally unjust that the undeserving should be crowned as that the undeserving should be damned.

We will conclude, therefore, that God ought to justify from *merit preceding*, or we will declare Him to be unjust, as being one who delights in evil and wicked men, and who invites and crowns their impiety by rewards.—And then, woe unto you, sensibly miserable sinners, under that God! For who among you can be saved! Behold, therefore, the iniquity of the human heart! When God saves the undeserving without merit, nay, justifies the impious with all their demerit, it does not accuse Him of iniquity, it does not expostulate with Him why He does it, although it is, in its own judgment, most iniquitous; but because it is to its own profit, and plausible, it considers it just and good. But when He damns the undeserving, this, because it is not to its own profit, is iniquitous; this is intolerable; here it expostulates, here it murmurs, here it blasphemes!

You see, therefore, that the Diatribe, together with its friends, do not, in this cause, judge according to equity, but according to the feeling sense of their own profit. For, if they regarded equity, they would expostulate with God when He crowned the undeserving, as they expostulate with Him when He damns the undeserving. And also, they would equally praise and proclaim God when He damns the undeserving, as they do when He saves the undeserving; for the iniquity in either instance is the same, if our own opinion be regarded:—unless they mean to say, that the iniquity is not equal, whether you laud Cain for his fratricide and make him a king, or cast the innocent Abel into prison and murder him!

Since, therefore, Reason praises God when He saves the undeserving, but accuses Him when He damns the undeserving; it stands convicted of not praising God as God, but as a certain one who serves its own profit; that is, it seeks in God, itself and the things of itself, but seeks not God and the things of God. But if it be pleased with a God who crowns the undeserving, it ought not to be displeased with a God who damns the undeserving. For if He be just in the one instance, how shall He not be just in the other? seeing that, in the one instance, He pours forth grace and mercy upon the undeserving, and in the other, pours forth wrath and severity upon the undeserving?—He is, however, in both instances, monstrous and iniquitous in the sight of men; yet just and true in Himself. But, *how* it is just, that He should crown the undeserving, is incomprehensible now, but we shall see when we come there, where it will be no longer believed, but seen in revelation face to face. So also, *how* it is just, that He should damn the undeserving, is incomprehensible now, yet, we believe it, until the Son of Man shall be revealed! [94]

CHAPTER 20:
THE TOTAL DEPRAVITY OF ALL MEN

Total depravity, total enslavement to sin, proves that man does not have free will. All the arguments of man in defense of free will are vain. True scholarship reveals that man has always fallen short of the glory of God. There is absolutely no part of man prior to the new birth which has any goodness in it or ability to seek after God or to please God.

86. ANOTHER passage is that of Gen. 8:21, "The thought and imagination of man's heart, is evil from his youth." And that also Gen. 6:5, "Every imagination of man's heart is only evil continually." These passages it evades thus:—"The proneness to evil which is in most men, does not, wholly, take away the freedom of the will."

Does God, I pray you, here speak of 'most men,' and not rather of all men, when, after the flood, as it were repenting, He promises to those who were then remaining, and to those who were to come, that He would no more bring a flood upon the earth "for man's sake:" assigning this as the reason:—because man is prone to evil! As though He had said, If I should act according to the wickedness of man, I should never cease from bringing a flood. Wherefore, henceforth, I will not act according to *that which he deserves,*. . . You see, therefore, that God, both before and after the flood, declares that man is evil: so that what the Diatribe says about 'most men,' amounts to nothing at all. Moreover, a proneness or inclination to evil, appears to the Diatribe, to be a matter of little moment; as though it were in our own power to keep ourselves upright, or to restrain it: whereas the Scripture, by that proneness, signifies the continual bent and evil impelling force of the will, to evil. Why does not the Diatribe here appeal to the Hebrew? Moses says nothing there about proneness. But, that you may have no

room for fussing over details, the Hebrew, (Gen. 6:5), runs thus:—"CHOL IETZER MAHESCHEBOTH LIBBO RAK RA CHOL HAIOM:" that is, "Every imagination of the thought of the heart is only evil all days." He does not say, that he is intent or prone to evil; but that, evil altogether, and nothing but evil, is thought or imagined by man throughout his whole life. The nature of his evil is described to be that which neither does nor can do anything but evil, as being evil itself: for, according to the testimony of Christ, an evil tree can bring forth none other than evil fruit. (Matt. 7:17-18).

And as to the Diatribe's pertly objecting—"Why was time given for repentance, then, if no part of repentance depends on Freewill, and all things are conducted according to the law of necessity."—

I answer: You may make the same objection to all the precepts of God; and say, Why does He command at all, if all things take place of necessity? He commands, in order to instruct and admonish, that men, being humbled under the knowledge of their evil, might come to grace, as I have fully shown already.—This passage, therefore, still remains invincible against the freedom of the will! [95]

87. THE fourth passage is that of Isaiah in the same chapter. "All flesh is grass, and all the glory of it as the flower of grass: the grass is withered, the flower of grass is fallen: because the Spirit of the Lord hath blown upon it." (Isa. 40:6-7). . . . Isaiah, who interprets his own meaning in his own words, saying, "Surely the people is grass?" He does not say; Surely the infirm condition of man is grass, but "the people;" and affirms it with a strong assertion. And what is the people? Is it the infirm condition of man only? —BUT let us . . . take Isaiah's words as they are. "The people (he says) is grass." "People" does not signify flesh merely, or the infirm condition of human nature, but it comprehends everything that there is in people—the rich, the wise, the just, the saints. Unless you mean to say, that the pharisees, the elders, the princes, the nobles, and the rich men, were not of the people of the

Jews! The "flower of grass" is rightly called their glory, because it was in their kingdom, their government, and above all, in the Law, in God, in righteousness, and in wisdom, that they gloried: as Paul shows, Rom. 2, 3 and 9.

When, therefore, Isaiah says, "All flesh," what else does he mean but all "grass," or, all "people?" For he does not say "flesh" only, but "all flesh." And to "people" belong soul, body, mind, reason, judgment, and whatever is called or found to be most excellent in man. For when he says "all flesh is grass," he excepts nothing but the Spirit which withers it and causes it to fade away. Nor does he omit anything when he says, "the people is grass." Speak, therefore, of "Freewill," speak of anything that can be called the highest or the lowest in the people,—Isaiah calls the whole "flesh and grass!" Because, those three terms "flesh," "grass," and "people," according to his interpretation who is himself the writer of the book, signify in that place, the same thing. . . . You have here Isaiah, who cries with a loud voice that the people, devoid of the Spirit of the Lord, is "flesh;" although you will not understand him thus. You have also your own confession, where you said, (though unwittingly perhaps), that the wisdom of the Greeks was "grass," or the glory of grass; which is the same thing as saying, it was "flesh."—Unless you mean to say, that the wisdom of the Greeks did not pertain to reason, or to the EGEMONICON, as you say, that is, *the principal part of man*. If, therefore, you will not deign to listen to me, listen to yourself; where, being caught in the powerful trap of truth, you speak the truth.

You have moreover the testimony of John, "That which is born of the flesh is flesh, and that which is born of the Spirit is spirit." (John 3:6). You have, I say, this passage, which makes it evidently manifest, that what is not born of the Spirit, is flesh: for if it be not so, the distinction of Christ could not subsist, who divides all men into two distinct divisions, "flesh" and "spirit."

". . . we most abundantly prove that though it is not found in the

Scriptures, that one detached portion, or 'that which is most excellent,' or the 'principal part,' of man is flesh, but that the whole of man is flesh! And not only so, but that the whole people is flesh! And further still, that the whole human race is flesh! For Christ says, "That which is born of the flesh is flesh." ... We do not believe only, but we see and experience, that the whole human race is "*born* of the flesh;" and therefore, we are compelled to believe upon the Word of Christ, that which we do not see; that the whole human race "*is* flesh."

AND as to your saying—"Yet every affection of man is not flesh. There is an affection called soul: there is an affection called spirit: by which we aspire to what is meritoriously good, as the philosophers aspired: who taught, that we should rather die a thousand deaths than commit one base action, even though we were assured that men would never know it and that God would pardon it."—

I answer: He who believes nothing certainly, may easily believe and say any thing. I will not ask you, but let your friend Lucian ask you, whether you can bring forward anyone out of the whole human race, let him be twice or seven times greater than Socrates himself, whoever performed this of which you speak, and which you say they taught. Why then do you thus babble in vanities of words? Could they ever aspire to that which is meritoriously good, who did not even know what good is?

If I should ask you for some of the brightest examples of your meritorious good deeds, you would say, perhaps, that it was meritoriously good when men died for their country, for their wives and children, and for their parents; or when they refrained from lying, or from treachery; or when they endured exquisite torments, as did Q. Scevola, M. Regulus, and others. But what can you point out in all those men, but an external show of works. For did you ever see their hearts? Nay, it was manifest from the very appearance of their works, that they did all these things for their own glory; so much so, that they were not even ashamed to confess and to boast that they sought their own glory.

For the Romans, according to their own testimonies, did whatever they did of virtue or valour, from a thirst after glory. The same did the Greeks, the same did the Jews, the same do all the race of men.

But though this be meritoriously good before men, yet, before God nothing is less meritoriously good than all this; nay, it is most impious, and the greatest of sacrilege; because, they did it not for the glory of God, nor that they might glorify God, but with the most impious of all robbery. For as they were robbing God of His glory and taking it to themselves, they never were farther from meritorious good, never more base, than when they were shining in their most exalted virtues. How could they do what they did for the glory of God, when they neither knew God nor His glory? Not, however, because it did not appear, but because the "flesh" did not permit them to see the glory of God, from their fury and madness after their own glory. This, therefore, is that right-ruling 'spirit,' that 'principal part of man, which aspires to what is meritoriously good'—it is a plunderer of the divine glory, and an usurper of the divine Majesty! and then the most so, when men are at the highest of their meritorious good, and the most glittering in their brightest virtues! Deny, therefore, if you can, that these are "flesh" and carried away by an impious affection.

Unless, perhaps, the Diatribe should still make this remaining query—Supposing the whole of man to be "flesh," and that which is most excellent in man to be called "flesh," must therefore that which is called "flesh" be at once called ungodly?—I call him ungodly who is without the Spirit of God. For the Scripture says, that the Spirit was therefore given, that He might justify the ungodly. And as Christ makes a distinction between the spirit and the flesh, saying, "That which is born of the flesh is flesh," and adds, that that which is born of the flesh "cannot see the kingdom of God" (John 3:3-6), it evidently follows, that whatever is flesh is ungodly, under the wrath of God, and a stranger to the kingdom of God. And if it be a stranger to the kingdom of God it necessarily follows that it is under the kingdom and spirit of Satan. For there is no *middle ground* between the kingdom of God and the kingdom of Satan; they are mutually and eternally opposed to each other.

These are the arguments that prove that the most exalted virtues among the nations, the highest perfections of the philosophers, and the greatest excellencies among men, appear indeed, in the sight of men, to be meritoriously virtuous and good, and are so called; but that, in the sight of God, they are in truth "flesh," and subservient to the kingdom of Satan: that is, ungodly, sacrilegious, and, in every respect, evil!

BUT pray let us suppose the sentiment of the Diatribe to stand good—'that every affection is not "flesh;" that is, ungodly; but is that which is called good and sound spirit.'—Only observe what absurdity must hence follow; not only with respect to human reason, but with respect to the Christian religion, and the most important Articles of Faith. For if that which is most excellent in man be not ungodly, nor utterly depraved, nor damnable, but that which is flesh only, that is the grosser and viler affections, what sort of a Redeemer shall we make Christ? Shall we rate the price of His blood so low as to say that it redeemed that part of man only which is the most vile, and that the most excellent part of man has power to work its own salvation, and does not want Christ? Henceforth then, I must preach Christ as the Redeemer, not of the whole man, but of his vilest part; that is, of his flesh; but that the man himself is his own redeemer, in his better part!

Have it, therefore, whichever way you will. If the better part of man be sound, it does not want Christ as a Redeemer. And if it does not want Christ, it triumphs in a glory above that of Christ: for it takes care of the redemption of the better part itself, whereas Christ only takes care of that of the vile part. And then, moreover, the kingdom of Satan will come to nothing at all, for it will reign only in the viler part of man, because the man himself will rule over the better part.

So that, by this doctrine of yours, concerning 'the principal part of man,' it will come to pass, that man will be exalted above Christ and the devil both: that is, he will be made God of gods, and Lord of lords!—Where is now that 'probable opinion' which asserted 'that "Freewill" cannot will anything good?' It here contends, 'that it is a principal part, meritoriously good, and sound; and that, it does not even want Christ, but can do more than God Himself and the devil can do, put together!

I say this, that you may again see, how eminently perilous a matter it is to attempt to discuss sacred and divine things, without the Spirit of God, in the utter vanity of human reason. If, therefore, Christ be the Lamb of God that takes away the sins of the world, it follows, that the whole world is under sin, damnation, and the devil. Hence your distinction between the *principal parts*, and the parts *not principal*, profits you nothing: for the *world*, signifies *men, savouring of nothing but the things of the world, throughout all their faculties.*

I make a manifest distinction between "flesh" and "spirit," as things that directly militate against each other; and I say, according to the divine oracles, that the man who is not regenerated by faith "is flesh;" but I say, that he who is thus regenerated; is no longer flesh, excepting as to the remnants of the flesh, which war against the first fruits of the Spirit received. [96]

88. Where now then remains that article of our faith; that Satan is the prince of the world, and, according to the testimonies of Christ and Paul, rules in the wills and minds of those men who are his captives and servants? Shall that roaring lion, that implacable and ever-restless enemy of the grace of God and the salvation of man, allow it to be, that man, his slave and a part of his kingdom, should attempt good by any motion in any degree, whereby he might escape from his tyranny, and that he should not rather spur and urge him on to will and do the contrary to grace with all his powers? especially when the just, and those who are led by the Spirit of God, and who will and do good, can hardly resist him, so great is his rage against them?

You who conceive that the human will is a something placed in a *free middle ground,* and left to itself, certainly conceive at the same time, that there is an endeavour which can exert itself either way; because, you make both God and the devil to be at a distance, spectators only, as it were, of this mutable and "Freewill"; though you do not believe that they are impellers and agitators of that enslaved will, the most hostilely opposed to each other.

Admitting, therefore, this part of your faith only, my sentiment stands firmly established, and "Freewill" lies prostrate; as I have shown already.—For, it must either be, that the kingdom of Satan in man is nothing at all, and thus Christ will be made to lie; or, if his kingdom be such as Christ describes, "Freewill" must be nothing but a beast of burden, the captive of Satan, which cannot be liberated unless the devil be first cast out by the finger of God. . . .

First of all then I will make that evidently manifest, which is plainly proved by Scriptures neither ambiguous nor obscure,—that Satan, is by far the most powerful and crafty prince of this world; (as I said before,) under the reigning power of whom, the human will, being no longer free nor in its own power, but the servant of sin and of Satan, can will nothing but that which its prince wills. And he will not permit it to will anything good: though, even if Satan did not reign over it, sin itself, of which man is the slave, would sufficiently harden it to prevent it from willing good. . . .

For I say, that man without the grace of God, remains, nevertheless, under the general Omnipotence of an acting God, who moves and carries along all things, of necessity, in the course of His infallible motion; but that the man's being thus carried along, is nothing; that is, avails nothing in the sight of God, nor is considered anything else but sin. . . .

I also know very well, that Paul cooperates with God in teaching the

Corinthians, so that he preaches to their intellects, while God teaches their spirits; and that, where their works are different. In like manner, he cooperates with God while he speaks by the Spirit of God; and that, where the work is the same. For what I assert and contend for is this:—that God, where He operates without the grace of His Spirit, works all in all, even in the ungodly; while He alone moves, acts on, and carries along by the motion of His omnipotence, all those things which He alone has created, which motion those things can neither avoid nor change, but of necessity follow and obey, each one according to the measure of power given of God:—thus all things, even the ungodly, cooperate with God! On the other hand, when He acts by the Spirit of His grace on those whom He has justified, that is, in His own kingdom, He moves and carries them along in the same manner; and they, as they are the new creatures, follow and cooperate with Him; or rather, as Paul says, are led by Him. (Rom. 8:14, 30.)

But the present is not the place for discussing these points. We are not now considering, what we can do in cooperation with God, but what we can do of ourselves: that is, whether, created as we are out of nothing, we can do or attempt anything of ourselves, under the general motion of God's omnipotence, whereby to prepare ourselves unto the new Creation of the Spirit.—This is the point to which Erasmus ought to have answered, and not to have turned aside to a something else!

What I have to say upon this point is this:—As man, before he is created man, does nothing and endeavours nothing towards his being made a creature; and as, after he is made and created, he does nothing and endeavours nothing towards his preservation, or towards his continuing in his creature-existence, but each takes place alone by the will of the omnipotent power and goodness of God, creating us and preserving us, without ourselves; but as . . .

God, nevertheless, does not work *in* us *without* us, seeing we are for that purpose created and preserved, that He might work in us and that we might cooperate with Him, whether it be out of

His kingdom under His general omnipotence, or in His kingdom under the distinct power of His Spirit. . .

so, man, before he is regenerated into the new creation of the kingdom of the Spirit, does nothing and endeavours nothing towards his new creation into that kingdom, and after he is recreated does nothing and endeavours nothing towards his perseverance in that kingdom; but the Spirit alone effects both in us, regenerating us and preserving us when regenerated, without ourselves; as James says, "Of His own will begat He us by the word of His power, that we should be a kind of first-fruits of His creatures,"—(Jas. 1:18) (where he speaks of the renewed creation:) nevertheless, He does not work *in* us *without* us, seeing that He has for this purpose created and preserved us, that He might operate in us, and that we might cooperate with Him:

thus, by us He preaches, shows mercy to the poor, and comforts the afflicted.—But what is hereby attributed to "Freewill?"Nay, what is there left it but nothing at all? And in truth it is nothing at all! . . .

READ therefore the Diatribe in this part through five or six pages, and you will find that by illustrations of this kind and by some of the most beautiful passages and parables selected from the Gospel and from Paul, it does nothing else but show us that innumerable passages (as it observes) are to be found in the Scriptures which speak of the cooperation and assistance of God: from which, if I should draw this conclusion—Man can do nothing without the assisting grace of God: therefore, no works of man are good—it would on the contrary conclude, as it has done by a rhetorical inversion—"Nay, there is nothing that man cannot do by the assisting grace of God: therefore, all the works of man can be good. For as many passages as there are in the Holy Scriptures which make mention of assistance, so many are there which confirm "Freewill;" and they are innumerable. Therefore, if we go by the number of testimonies, the victory is mine." Do you think the Diatribe could be sober or in its right senses when it wrote this? For I cannot attribute it to malice or iniquity: unless it be that it designed to effectually wear me out by perpetually wearying me, while thus, ever like itself, it is continually turning aside to something contrary to its professed design. But if it is pleased thus to play the fool in a matter so important, then I will be pleased to expose its voluntary tomfooleries publicly.

In the first place, I do not dispute, nor am I ignorant, that all the works of man *may be* good, if they be done by the assisting grace of God. And moreover that there is nothing which a man might not do by the assisting grace of God. But I cannot feel enough surprise at your negligence, who, having set out with the professed design to write upon the power of "Freewill," go on writing upon the power of grace. And moreover, dare to assert publicly, as if all men were posts or stones, that "Freewill" is established by those passages of Scripture which exalt the grace of God. And not only dare to do that, but even to sound forth congratulations on yourself as a victor most gloriously triumphant! From this very word and act of yours, I truly perceive what "Freewill" is, and what the effect of it is—it makes men mad! For what, I ask, can it be in you that talks at this rate, but "Freewill!"

But just listen to your own conclusions.—The Scripture commends the grace of God: therefore, it proves "Freewill."—It exalts the assistance of the grace of God: therefore, it establishes "Freewill." By what kind of logic did you learn such conclusions as these? On the contrary, why not conclude thus?—Grace is preached: therefore, "Freewill" has no existence. The assistance of grace is exalted: therefore, "Freewill" is abolished. For, to what intent is grace given? Is it for this: that "Freewill," as being of sufficient power itself, might proudly display and sport grace on holidays, as a gaudy ornament! Wherefore, I will invert your order of reasoning, and though no rhetorician, will establish a conclusion more firm than yours.—As many places as there are in the Holy Scriptures which make mention of assistance, so many are there which abolish "Freewill:" and they are innumerable. Therefore, if we are to go by the number of testimonies, the victory is mine. For grace is therefore needed, and the assistance of grace is therefore given, because "Freewill" can of itself do nothing; as Erasmus himself has asserted according to that 'probable opinion' that "Freewill" 'cannot will anything good.' Therefore, when grace is commended, and the assistance of grace declared, the impotency of "Freewill" is declared at the same time.—This is a sound inference—a firm conclusion—against which, not even the gates of hell will ever prevail!

HERE, I bring to a conclusion, THE DEFENSE OF MY SCRIPTURES WHICH THE DIATRIBE ATTEMPTED TO REFUTE; lest my book should be swelled to too great a volume: and if there be anything yet remaining that is worthy of notice, it shall be taken into THE FOLLOWING PART; WHEREIN, I MAKE MY ASSERTIONS. For as to what Erasmus says in his conclusion—'that, if my sentiments stand good, the numberless precepts, the numberless threatenings, the numberless promises, are all in vain, and no place is left for merit or demerit, for rewards or punishments; that moreover, it is difficult to defend the mercy, nay, even the justice of God, if God damn sinners of necessity; and that many other difficulties follow, which have so troubled some of the greatest men, as even to utterly overthrow them,'—

To all these things I have fully replied already. Nor will I receive or bear with that *moderate middle ground*, which Erasmus would (with a good intention, I believe,) recommend to me;—'that we should grant *some certain little* to "Freewill;" in order that the contradictions of the Scripture, and the difficulties before mentioned, might be the more easily remedied.'—For by this *moderate middle ground*, the matter is not bettered, nor is any advantage gained whatever. Because, unless you ascribe the whole and all things to "Freewill," as the Pelagians do, the 'contradictions' in the Scriptures are not altered, merit and reward are taken entirely away, the mercy and justice of God are abolished, and all the difficulties which we try to avoid by allowing this 'certain little ineffective power' to "Freewill," remain just as they were before; as I have already fully shown. Therefore, we must come to the plain extreme: deny "Freewill" altogether, and ascribe all unto God! Thus, there will be in the Scriptures no contradictions; and if there be any difficulties, they will be borne with, where they cannot be remedied.

THIS one thing, however, my friend Erasmus, I entreat of you—do not consider that I conduct this cause more according to my temper, than according to my principles. I will not allow it to be insinuated, that I am hypocrite enough to write one thing and believe another. I have not (as you say of me) been carried so far by the heat of defensive argument, as to 'deny here "Freewill" altogether for the first time, having conceded something to it before.' Confident I am, that you can find no such concession anywhere in my works. There are questions and discussions of mine extant, in which I have continued to assert, down to this hour, that there is no such thing as "Freewill;" that it is *a thing formed out of an empty term*; (which are the words I have there used). And I then thus believed and thus wrote, as overpowered by the force of truth when called and compelled to the discussion.

And as to my always conducting discussions with fervency, I acknowledge my fault, if it be a fault: nay, I greatly glory in this testimony which the world bears of me, in the cause of God: and may God Himself confirm the same testimony in the last day! Then, who more happy than Luther—to be honoured with the universal testimony of his age, that he did not maintain the Cause of Truth lazily, nor neglectfully, but with a real, if not too great, fervency! Then shall I be blessedly clear from that word of Jeremiah, "Cursed be he that doeth the work of the Lord negligently!" (Jer. 48:10). [97]

CHAPTER 21:

GOD'S WRATH TOWARD MAN IS FULLY JUSTIFIED

Man's works justify punishment. The Scriptures are all-inclusive in their condemnation of all men outside of Christ. God's way of righteousness is not only foreign to the natural man, natural man has never conceived of God's way of righteousness. The best performance of the very best of men is evil in God's sight. No one ever has and no one ever will endeavor after good (as defined by God) because even the concept of good (as defined by God) has never occurred to natural man, and will never occur to natural man. Natural man has never been able to either correctly define sin, or find a way to take sin away. Thus, man is helpless to find a way out of his lostness apart from God's grace and the hearing of the gospel. It is through total despair of finding a way out that God reveals his salvation to those He has chosen. The real meaning of grace, cheap grace, and costly grace. Final thrusts to defeat the concept of any kind of merit on man's part in obtaining the grace of God.

89. PAUL, writing to the Romans, thus enters upon his argument, *against* **Freewill, and for the grace of God. "The wrath of God (says he) is revealed from heaven against all ungodliness and unrighteousness of men, who hold down the truth in unrighteousness." (Rom. 1:18)**

Do you hear this general sentence "against all men,"—that they are all under the wrath of God? And what is this but declaring, that they all merit wrath and punishment? For he assigns the cause of the wrath against them—they do nothing but that which merits wrath; because they are all ungodly and unrighteous, and hold down, or suppress, the truth in unrighteousness. Where is now the power of "Freewill" which can endeavour anything good? Paul makes it to merit the wrath of God, and pronounces it ungodly and unrighteous. That, therefore, which

merits wrath and is ungodly, only endeavours and avails *against* grace, not *for* grace.. . . the words "against all ungodliness of men" are of the same import, as if you should say,—against the ungodliness of all men. For Paul, in almost all these instances, uses a Hebraism: so that, the sense is,—all men are ungodly and unrighteous, and hold down the truth in unrighteousness; and therefore, all merit wrath. Hence, in the Greek, there is no *relative* which might be rendered 'of those who,' but an *article*, causing the sense to run thus, "The wrath of God is revealed from heaven against all ungodliness and unrighteousness of men, holding the truth in unrighteousness." So that this may be taken as an epithet, as it were, applicable to all men as "holding the truth in unrighteousness:" . . .

THIS passage of Paul, therefore, stands firmly and forcibly urging—that "Freewill," even in its most exalted state, in the most exalted men, who were endowed with the Law, righteousness, wisdom, and all the virtues, was ungodly and unrighteous, and merited the wrath of God; or the argument of Paul amounts to nothing. And if it stand good, his division leaves no *middle ground*: for he makes those who believe the Gospel to be under the salvation of God, and all the rest to be under the wrath of God: he makes the believing to be righteous, and the unbelieving to be ungodly, unrighteous, and under wrath. For the whole that he means to say is this:—The righteousness of God is revealed in the Gospel, that it might be by faith. But God would be lacking in wisdom, if He should *reveal* righteousness unto men, when they either knew it already or had 'some seeds' of it themselves. Since, however, He is not lacking in wisdom, and yet reveals unto men the righteousness of salvation, it is manifest, that "Freewill" even in the most exalted of men, not only has wrought, and can work no righteousness, but does not even know what is righteous before God.—Unless you mean to say, that the righteousness of God is not revealed unto these most exalted of men, but to the most vile!—But the boasting of Paul is quite the contrary—that he is a debtor, both to the Jews and to the Greeks, to the wise and to the unwise, to the Greeks and to the barbarians.

Wherefore Paul, comprehending, in this passage, all men together in one mass, concludes that they are all ungodly, unrighteous, and ignorant of the righteousness of faith: so far is it from possibility, that they can will or do anything good. And this conclusion is moreover confirmed from this:—that God *reveals* the righteousness of faith to them, as being ignorant and sitting in darkness: therefore, of themselves, they know it not. And if they be ignorant of the righteousness of salvation, they are certainly under wrath and damnation: nor can they extricate themselves therefrom, nor *endeavour* to extricate themselves: for how can you endeavour, if you know neither what you are to endeavour after, nor in what way, nor to what extent, you are to endeavour?

WITH this conclusion both the thing itself and experience agree. For show me one of the whole race of mankind, be he the most holy and most just of all men, into whose mind it ever came, that the way unto righteousness and salvation, was to believe in Him who is both God and man, who died for the sins of men and rose again, and sits at the right hand of God the Father, that He might still that wrath of God the Father which Paul here says is revealed from heaven?

Look at the most eminent philosophers! What ideas had they of God! What have they left behind them in their writings concerning the wrath to come! Look at the Jews instructed by so many wonders and so many successive Prophets! What did they think of this way of righteousness? They not only did not receive it, but so hated it, that no nation under heaven has more atrociously persecuted Christ, unto this day. And who would dare to say, that in so great a people, there was not one who cultivated "Freewill," and endeavoured with all its power? How does it happen then, that they all endeavour in the directly opposite way, and that which was the most excellent in the most excellent men, not only did not follow this way of righteousness, not only did not know it, but even thrust it from them with the greatest hatred, and wished to destroy it when it was published and revealed? So much so, that Paul says this way was "to the Jews a stumbling-block, and to the Gentiles foolishness." (1 Cor. 1: 23.).

Since, therefore, Paul speaks of the Jews and Gentiles without difference, and since it is certain that the Jews and Gentiles include all the principal nations under heaven, it is hence certain, that "Freewill" is nothing else than the greatest enemy to righteousness and the salvation of man: for it is impossible, but that there must have been some among the Jews and Gentile Greeks who wrought and endeavoured with all the powers of "Freewill;" and yet, by all that endeavouring, did nothing but carry on a war against grace.

Do you therefore now come forward and say what "Freewill" can endeavour towards good, when goodness and righteousness themselves are a "stumbling-block" unto it, and "foolishness." Nor can you say that this applies to *some* and not to *all*. Paul speaks of all without difference, where he says, "to the Jews a stumbling-block and to the Gentiles foolishness:" nor does he except any but believers. "To us, (says he,) who are called, and saints, it is the power of God and wisdom of God." (1 Cor.1:24). He does not say to some Gentiles, to some Jews; but plainly, to the Gentiles and to the Jews, who are "not of us." Thus, by a manifest division, separating the believing from the unbelieving, and leaving no *middle ground* whatever. And we are now speaking of Gentiles as working without grace: to whom Paul says, the righteousness of God is "foolishness," and they abhor it.—This is that meritorious endeavour of "Freewill" towards good! . . .

If therefore, the most exalted and devoted endeavours and works in the most exalted of the nations be evil and ungodly, what shall we think of the rest, who are, as it were, the common people, and the vilest of the nations? Nor does Paul here make any difference between those who are the most exalted, for he condemns all the devotedness of their wisdom, without any respect of persons. And if he condemn their very works and devoted endeavours, he condemns those who exert them, even though they strive with all the powers of "Freewill." Their most exalted endeavour, I say, is declared to be evil—how much more then the persons themselves who exert it!

So also, just afterwards, he rejects the Jews, without any difference, who are Jews "in the letter" and not "in the spirit." "Thou (says he) honourest God in the letter, and in the circumcision." Again, "He is not a Jew which is one outwardly, but he is a Jew which is one inwardly." Rom. 1:27-29.

What can be more manifest than the division here made? The Jew outwardly, is a transgressor of the Law. And how many Jews must we suppose there were, without the faith, who were men the most wise, the most religious, and the most honourable, who aspired unto righteousness and truth with all the devotion of endeavour? Of these the apostle continually bears testimony:—that they had "a zeal of God," that they "followed after righteousness," that they strove day and night to attain unto salvation, that they lived "blameless:" and yet they are transgressors of the Law, because they are not Jews "in the spirit," nay they determinately resist the righteousness of faith. What conclusion then remains to be drawn, but that, "Freewill" is then the worst when it is the best; and that the more it endeavours, the worse it becomes, and the worse it is! The words are plain—the division is certain—nothing can be said against it. [98]

90. BUT let us hear Paul, who is his own interpreter. In the third chapter, drawing up, as it were, a conclusion, he says, "What then? are we better than they? No, in no wise; for we have before proved both Jews and Greeks that they are all under sin." (Rom. 3:9). Where is now "Freewill!" All, says he, both Jews and Greeks are under sin! Are there

any 'figures of speech' or 'difficulties' here? What would the 'invented interpretations' of the whole world do against this perfectly clear sentence? He who says "all," excepts none. And he who describes them all as being "under sin," that is, the servants of sin, leaves them no degree of good whatever. But where has he given this proof that "they are all, both Jews and Gentiles, under sin?" Nowhere, but where I have already shown: namely, where he says, "The wrath of God is revealed from heaven against all ungodliness and unrighteousness of men." This he proves to them afterwards from experience: showing them, that being hated of God, they were given up to so many vices, in order that they might be convinced from the fruits of their ungodliness, that they willed and did nothing but evil. And then he judges the Jews also separately; where he says, that the Jew "in the letter," is a transgressor of the Law: which he proves, in like manner, from the fruits, and from experience: saying, "Thou who declarest that a man should not steal, stealest thyself: thou who abhorrest idols, committest sacrilege." Thus excepting none whatever, but those who are Jews "in the spirit. . . .

How then can they endeavour toward good, who are all, without exception, ignorant of God, and neither regard nor seek after God? How can they have a power able to attain unto good, who all, without exception, decline from good and become utterly unprofitable? Are not the words most clear? And do they not declare this,—that all men are ignorant of God and despise God, and then, turn to evil and become unprofitable for good? For Paul is not here speaking of the ignorance of seeking food, or the contempt of money, but of the ignorance and contempt of religion and of godliness. And that ignorance and contempt, most undoubtedly, are not in the "flesh," that is, (as you interpret it,) 'the inferior and grosser affections,' but in the most exalted and most noble powers of man, in which, righteousness, godliness, the knowledge and reverence of God, ought to reign; that is, in the reason and in the will; and thus, in the very power of "Freewill," in the very seed of good, in that which is the most excellent in man! . . .

For what is it to be "unrighteous," but for the will, (which is one of the most noble faculties in man,) to be unrighteous? What is it to understand nothing either of God or good, but for the reason (which is another of the most noble faculties in man) to be ignorant of God and good, that is, to be blind to the knowledge of godliness? What is it to be "gone out of the way," and to have become unprofitable, but for men to have no power in one single faculty, and the least power in their most noble faculties, to turn unto good, but only to turn unto evil! What is it not to fear God, but for men to be in all their faculties, and most of all in their noblest faculties, despisers of all the things of God, of His words, His works, His laws, His precepts, and His will! What then can reason propose, that is right, who is thus blind and ignorant? What can the will choose that is good, which is thus evil and impotent? Nay, what can the will pursue, where the reason can propose nothing, but the darkness of its own blindness and ignorance? And where the reason is thus erroneous, and the will opposed, what can the man either do or attempt, that is good! . . .

BUT perhaps someone may, here sophistically observe—though the will be gone out of the way, and the reason be ignorant, as to the perfection of the act, yet the will can make some attempt, and the reason can attain to some knowledge by its own powers; seeing that we can attempt many things which we cannot perfect; and we are here speaking of the existence of a power, not of the perfection of the act.

I answer: The words of the Prophet comprehend both the *act* and the *power*. For his saying, man seeks not God, is the same as if he had said, man *cannot* seek God: which you may collect from this.—If there were a power or ability in man to will good, it could not be, but that, as the motion of the Divine Omnipotence could not allow it to remain actionless, or to keep holiday, (as I before observed) it must be moved forth into action in some men, at least in some one man or other, and must be made manifest so as to afford an example. But this is not the case. For God looks down from heaven, and does not see even one who seeks after Him, or attempts it. Wherefore it follows, that that power is nowhere to be found, which attempts, or wills to attempt, to seek after Him; and that all men "are gone out of the way."

Moreover if Paul be not understood to speak at the same time of impotency, his disputation will amount to nothing. For Paul's whole design is to make grace necessary unto all men. Whereas, if they could make some sort of beginning themselves, grace would not be necessary. But now, since they cannot make that beginning, grace is necessary. Hence you see that "Freewill" is by this passage utterly abolished, and nothing meritorious or good whatever left in man: seeing that he is declared to be unrighteous, ignorant of God, a despiser of God, opposed to God, and unprofitable in the sight of God. And the words of the prophet are sufficiently forcible both in their own place, and in Paul who quotes them.

Nor is it an inconsiderable assertion, when man is said to be ignorant of, and to despise God: for these are the fountain springs of all iniquities, the cesspool of all sins, and the hell of all evils. What evil is there not, where there are ignorance and contempt of God? In a word, the whole kingdom of Satan in men, could not be defined in fewer or more expressive words than by saying—they are ignorant of and despise God! For there is unbelief, there is disobedience, there is sacrilege, there is blasphemy against God, there is cruelty and a lack of mercy towards our neighbour, there is the love of self in all the things of God and man!—Here you have a description of the glory and power of "Freewill!"

PAUL however proceeds; and testifies that he now expressly speaks with reference to all men, and to those more especially who are the greatest and most exalted: saying, "that every mouth may be stopped, and all the world become guilty before God: for by the works of the Law shall no flesh be justified in His sight." (Rom. 3:19-20). [99]

91. For Paul is here speaking, principally, to the Jews, as he says, Rom. 1: wherefore, let no one doubt, that by the works of the Law here, all the works of the whole Law are to be understood. For if the Law be abolished and dead, they cannot be called the works of the Law; for an abolished or dead Law, is no longer a law; and that Paul knew full well. Therefore, he does not speak of the Law abolished, when he speaks of the works of the Law, but of the Law in force and authority: otherwise, how easy would it have been for him to say, The Law is now abolished? And then, he would have spoken openly and clearly.

But let us bring forward Paul himself, who is the best interpreter of his own words. He says, Gal. 3:10, "As many as are of the works of the Law, are under the curse; for it is written, Cursed is every one that continueth not in all things, which are written in the book of the Law, to do them." You see that Paul here, where he is urging the same point as he is in his epistle to the Romans, and in the same words, speaks, wherever he makes mention of the works of the Law, of all the laws that are written in the Book of the Law.

And what is still more worthy of remark, Paul himself cites Moses, who curses those that *continue not* in the Law; whereas, he himself curses those who *are of* the works of the Law; thus producing a testimony of a different scope from that of his own sentiment; the former being in the negative, the latter in the affirmative. But this he does, because the real state of the case is such in the sight of God, that those who are the most devoted to the works of the Law, are the farthest from fulfilling the Law, as being without the Spirit, who only is the fulfiller of the Law, which such may attempt to fulfill by their own powers, but they will effect nothing after all. Wherefore, both declarations are truth—that of Moses, that they are accursed who *continue not* in the works of the Law; and that of Paul, that they are accursed who *are of* the works of the Law.

For both characters of persons require the Spirit, without which, the works of the Law, no matter how many and excellent they may be, justify not, as Paul says; wherefore neither character of persons *continue in* all things that are written, as Moses says.

IN a word: Paul by this division of his, fully confirms that which I maintain. For he divides Law-working men into two classes, those who work by the power of the Spirit, and those who work by the power of the flesh, leaving no *middle ground* whatever. He speaks thus: "By the deeds of the Law shall no flesh be justified." (Rom. 3:20). What is this but saying, that those whose works profit them not, work the works of the Law without the power of the Spirit, as being themselves flesh; that is, unrighteous and ignorant of God. So, Gal. 3: 2, making the same division, he says, "received ye the Spirit by the works of the Law, or by the hearing of faith?" Again Rom. 3:21, "but now, the righteousness of God is manifest without the Law." And again Rom. 3:28, "We conclude, therefore, that a man is justified by faith without *[or, apart from]* the works of the Law."

From all of which it is manifest and clear, that in Paul, the Spirit is set in opposition to the works of the Law, as well as to all other things which are not spiritual, including all the powers of, and every thing pertaining to the flesh. So that the meaning of Paul is evidently the same as that of Christ, John 3:6, that every thing which is not of the Spirit is flesh, be it ever so deceptively attractive, holy and great, nay, be they works of the divine Law the most excellent, and wrought by all the powers imaginable; for the Spirit of Christ is lacking; without which, all things are nothing short of being damnable.

Let it then be a settled point that Paul, by the works of the Law, means not the ceremonial works, but the works of the *whole* Law; then, this will be a settled point also, that in the works of the Law, everything is condemned that is without the Spirit. And without the Spirit, is that power of "Freewill," (for that is the point in dispute),—that most exalted faculty in man! For, to be "of the works of the Law," is the most exalted state in which man can be. The apostle therefore does not say who are of sins, and of ungodliness against the Law, but who are "of the works of the Law;" that is, who are the best of men, and the most devoted to the Law: and who are, in addition to the power of "Freewill," even assisted, that is, instructed and roused into action, by the Law itself.

If therefore "Freewill" assisted by the Law and exercising all its powers in the Law, profit nothing and justify not, but be left in sin and in the flesh, what must we suppose it able to do, when left to itself without the Law!

"By the Law (says Paul) is the knowledge of sin." (Rom. 3:20). Here he shows how much, and how far the Law profits:—that "Freewill" is of itself so blind, that it does not even know what is sin, but has need of the Law for its teacher.

> And what can that man do towards taking away sin, who does not even know what is sin? All that he can do is to mistake that which is sin for that which is no sin, and that which is no sin for that which is sin.

And this, experience sufficiently proves true. How does the world, by the middle ground of those whom it accounts the most excellent and the most devoted to righteousness and piety, hate and persecute the righteousness of God preached in the Gospel, and brand it with the name of heresy, error, and every shameful appellation, while it boasts of and sets forth its own works and devices, which are really sin and error, as righteousness and wisdom? By this Scripture, therefore, Paul stops the mouth of "Freewill" where he teaches that by the Law its sin is clearly manifested to it, of which sin it was previously ignorant; so far is he from conceding to it any power whatever to attempt that which is good. [100]

---

92. AND here is solved that question of the Diatribe so often repeated throughout its book—"if we can do nothing, to what purpose are so many laws, so many precepts, so many threatenings, and so many promises?"—

Paul here gives an answer: "By the Law is the knowledge of sin." His answer is far different from that which would enter the thoughts of man, or of "Freewill." He does not say, by the Law is proved "Freewill," because it cooperates with it unto righteousness. For righteousness is not by the Law, but, "by the Law is the knowledge of sin:" seeing that the effect, the work, and the office of the Law, is to be a light to the ignorant and the blind; such a light, as makes known to them disease, sin, evil, death, hell, and the wrath of God; though it does not deliver from these, but shows them only.

> And when a man is thus brought to a knowledge of the disease of sin, he is cast down, is afflicted, nay despairs: the Law does not help him, much less can he help himself. Another light is necessary, which might make known to him the remedy. This is the voice of the Gospel, revealing Christ as the Deliverer from all these evils.

Neither "Freewill" nor reason can discover Him. And how should it discover Him, when it is itself dark and devoid even of the light of the Law, which might make known to it its disease, which disease, in its own light it sees not, but believes it to be sound health.

So also in Galatians 3, treating on the same point, he says, "Wherefore then serveth the Law?" To which he answers, not as the Diatribe does, in a way that proves the existence of "Freewill," but he says, "it was added because of transgressions, until the Seed should come, to whom the promise was made." (Gal. 3:19). He says, "because of transgressions;" not, however, to restrain them, as Jerome dreams; (for Paul shows, that to take away and to restrain sins, by the gift of righteousness, was that which was promised to the Seed to come;) but to cause transgressions to abound, as he says Rom. 5:20, "The Law entered that sin might abound." Not that sins were not committed and did not abound without the Law, but they were not known to be transgressions and sins of such magnitude; for the most and greatest of them, were considered to be righteousnesses. And while sins are thus unknown, there is no place for remedy. or for hope; because, they will not submit to the hand of the healer, considering themselves to be whole, and not to need a physician. Therefore, the Law is necessary, which might give the knowledge of sin; in order that, he who is proud and whole in his own eyes, being humbled down into the knowledge of the iniquity and greatness of his sin, might groan and breathe after the grace that is laid up in Christ.

Only observe, therefore, the simplicity of the words—"By the Law is the knowledge of sin;" and yet, these alone are of force sufficient to confound and overthrow "Freewill" altogether. For if it be true, that of itself, it knows not what is sin, and what is evil, as the apostle says here, and Rom. 7:7-8, "I should not have known that concupiscence *[that is, looking at someone with sexual lust or at some thing with hot desire to possess it]* was sin, except the Law had said, Thou shalt not covet," how can it ever know what is righteousness and good? And if it know not what righteousness is, how can it endeavour to attain unto it? We know not the sin in which we were born, in which we live, in which we move and exist, and which lives, moves, and reigns in us; how then should we know that righteousness which is outside of us, and which reigns in heaven? These works bring that miserable thing "Freewill" to nothing—nothing at all!

THE state of the case, therefore, being thus, Paul speaks openly with full confidence and authority, saying, "But now the righteousness of God is manifest without the Law, being witnessed by the Law and the prophets; even the righteousness of God which is by faith of Jesus Christ unto all and upon all them that believe in Him: (for there is no difference, for all have sinned and are without the glory of God:) being justified freely by His grace through the redemption that is in Christ Jesus: Whom God hath set forth to be a propitiation for sin, through faith in His blood . . ." (Rom. 3:22-26).

Here Paul speaks forth mighty thunderbolts against "Freewill." First, he says, "The righteousness of God without the Law is manifested." Here he marks the distinction between the righteousness of God, and the righteousness of the Law: because, the righteousness of faith comes by grace, apart from the Law. His saying, "apart from the Law," can mean nothing else but that Christian righteousness exists apart from the works of the Law: inasmuch as the works of the Law avail nothing, and can do nothing, toward the attainment unto it. As he afterwards says, "Therefore we conclude that a man is justified by faith apart from the deeds of the Law." (Rom. 3:28). The same also he had said before, "By the deeds of the Law shall no flesh be justified in His sight." (Rom. 3:20).

From all of which it is most clearly manifest, that the endeavour and desire of "Freewill" are nothing at all. For if the righteousness of God exists apart from the Law, and apart from the works of the Law, how shall it not much rather exist apart from "Freewill"! especially, since the most devoted effort of "Freewill" is to exercise itself in moral righteousness, or the works of that Law, from which its blindness and impotency derive their 'assistance!' These words "apart from," therefore abolish all moral works, abolish all moral righteousness, abolish all preparations unto grace. In a word, scrape together every thing you can as that which pertains to the ability of "Freewill," and Paul will still stand invincible saying,—the righteousness of God is "entirely and absolutely apart from" it!

But, to grant that "Freewill" can by its endeavour, move itself in some direction, we will say, unto good works, or unto the righteousness of the civil or moral law; yet, it is not moved toward the righteousness of God, nor does God in any respect allow its devoted efforts to be worthy unto the attainment of this righteousness: for He says, that His righteousness exists *[in those who are counted righteous by God, entirely]* apart from the works of the Law. If therefore, it cannot move itself unto the attainment of the righteousness of God, what will it be profited, if it move itself by its own works and endeavours, unto the attainment of (if it were possible) the righteousness of angels! Here, I presume, the words are not 'obscure or ambiguous,' nor is any place left for 'figures of speech' of any kind. Here Paul distinguishes most manifestly the two righteousnesses; assigning the one to the Law, the other to grace; and declares that the latter is given apart from the former, and apart from its works; and that the former justifies not, nor avails anything, apart from the latter. I should like to see, therefore, how "Freewill" can stand, or be defended, against these Scriptures!

ANOTHER thunderbolt is this—The apostle says, that the righteousness of God is manifested in, and is available, "unto all and upon all them that believe" in Christ: and that, "there is no difference." (Rom. 3: 21-22).—

Here again, he divides in the clearest words, the whole race of men into two distinct divisions. To the believing he gives the righteousness of God, but takes it from the unbelieving. Now, no one, I suppose, will be madman enough to doubt, whether or not the power or endeavour of "Freewill" be a something that is not faith in Christ Jesus. Paul then denies that anything which is not this faith, is righteous before God. And if it be not righteous before God, it must be sin. For there is with God no *middle ground* between righteousness and sin, which can be as it were a *neuter*—neither righteousness nor sin. Otherwise the whole argument of Paul would amount to nothing: for it proceeds wholly upon this distinct division—that whatever is done and carried on by men, must be in the sight of God, either righteousness or sin: righteousness, if done in faith; sin, if faith be lacking. With men, indeed, things pass thus.—All cases in which men, in their interaction with each other, neither owe anything as a due, nor do anything as a free benefit, are called *middle ground* and neuter.

> But here the ungodly man sins against God, whether he eats, or
> whether he drinks, or whatever he does; because, he abuses the
> creation of God by his ungodliness and perpetual ingratitude,
> and does not, at any one moment, give glory to God from his
> heart.

THIS also, is no powerless thunderbolt where the apostle says, "All
have sinned and are without the glory of God: for there is no
difference." (Rom. 3:23).

What, I pray you, could be spoken more clearly? Produce one of
your "Freewill" workmen, and say to me—does this man sin in this his
endeavour? If he does not sin, why does not Paul except him? Why does
he include him also without difference? Surely he that says "all,"
excepts no one in any place, at any time, in any work or endeavour. If
therefore you except any man, for any kind of devoted desire or
work,—you make Paul a liar; because he includes that "Freewill"
workman or striver, among all the rest, and in all that he says
concerning them; whereas, Paul should have had some respect for this
person, and not have numbered him among the general herd of sinners!

There is also that part, where he says, that they are "without the
glory of God."

You may understand "the glory of God" here two ways, *actively* and
passively. For Paul writes thus from his frequent use of Hebraisms.
"The glory of God," understood actively, is that glory by which God
glories in us; understood passively, it is that glory by which we glory in
God. But it seems to me proper, to understand it now, passively. So,
"the faith of Christ," is, according to the Latin, the faith which Christ
has; but, according to the Hebrew, "the faith of Christ," is the faith
which we have in Christ. So, also, "the righteousness of God," signifies,
according to the Latin, the righteousness which God has; but according

to the Hebrew, it signifies the righteousness which we have from God and before God. Thus also "the glory of God," we understand according to the Latin, not according to the Hebrew; and receive it as signifying, the glory which we have from God and before God; which may be called, our glory in God.

> And that man glories in God who knows, to a certainty, that God looks with favor upon him, and deigns to look upon him with kind regard; and that, whatever he does pleases God, and what does not please him, is borne with by Him and pardoned.

If therefore, the endeavour or desire of "Freewill" be not sin, but good before God, it can certainly glory; and in that glorying, say with confidence,—This pleases God, God favors this, God looks upon and accepts this, or at least, bears with it and pardons it. For this is the glorying of the faithful in God: and they that have not this are rather confounded before God. But Paul here denies that these men have this; saying, that they are all entirely without this glory.

Our experience proves this.—Put the question to all the exercisers of "Freewill" to a man, and see if you can show me one who can honestly, and from his heart, say of any one of his devoted efforts and endeavours,—This pleases God! If you can bring forward a single one, I am ready to acknowledge myself overthrown, and to cede to you the palm. But I know there is not one to be found. And if this glory be lacking, so that the conscience dares not say, to a certainty, and with confidence,—this pleases God, it is certain that it does not please God. For as a man believes, so it is unto him: because, he does not, to a certainty, believe that he pleases God; which, nevertheless, it is necessary to believe; for to doubt of the favor of God, is the very sin itself of unbelief; because, He will have it believed with the most assuring faith that He is favorable. Therefore, I have convinced them upon the testimony of their own conscience, that "Freewill," being "without the glory of God," is, with all its powers, its devoted strivings

---

and endeavours, perpetually under the guilt of the sin of unbelief.

And what will the advocates of "Freewill" say to that which follows, "being justified freely by His grace?" (Rom. 3:24). What is the meaning of the word "freely?" What is the meaning of "by His grace?" How will merit and endeavour, accord with freely-given righteousness? But, perhaps, they will here say that they attribute to "Freewill" *a very little indeed*, and that which is by no means the 'merit of worthiness' (*meritum condignum!*) These, however, are mere empty words: for all that is sought for in the defense of "Freewill," is to make place for *merit*. This is manifest: for the Diatribe has, throughout, argued and expostulated thus, —

"If there be no freedom of will, how can there be place for merit? And if there be no place for merit, how can there be place for reward? To whom will the reward be assigned, if justification be without merit?

Paul here gives you an answer.—That there is no such thing as merit at all; but that all who are justified are justified "freely;" that this is ascribed to no one but to the grace of God.—And when this righteousness is given, the kingdom and life eternal are given with it! Where is your endeavouring now? Where is your devoted effort? Where are your works? Where are your merits of "Freewill?" Where is the profit of them all put together? You cannot here make, as a pretence, 'obscurity and ambiguity:' the facts and the works are most clear and most plain. It may be that they attribute to "Freewill" a very little indeed, yet they teach us that by that very little we can attain unto righteousness and grace. Nor do they solve that question, *Why does God justify one and leave another?* in any other way than by asserting the freedom of the will, and saying, *Because the one endeavours and the other does not: and God regards the one for his endeavouring and despises the other for his not endeavouring; lest, if he did otherwise, He should appear to be unjust.*

And notwithstanding all their pretence, both by their tongue and pen, that they do not profess to attain unto grace by 'the merit of worthiness' (*meritum condignum*) nor call it the merit of worthiness, yet they only mock us with a term, and hold fast their tenet all the while. For what is the amount of their pretence that they do not call it 'the merit of worthiness,' if nevertheless they assign unto it all that belongs to the merit of worthiness?—saying, that he in the sight of God attains unto grace who endeavours, and he who does not endeavour, does not attain unto it? Is this not plainly making it to be the merit of worthiness? Is it not making God a respecter of works, of merits, and of persons to say that one man is devoid of grace from his own fault, because he did not endeavour after it, but that another, because he did endeavour after it, has attained unto grace, unto which he would not have attained, if he had not endeavoured after it? If this be not 'the merit of worthiness,' then I should like to be informed what it is that is called 'the merit of worthiness.'

In this way you may play a game of mockery upon all words; and say, it is not indeed the merit of worthiness, but is in effect the same as the 'merit of worthiness.'—The thorn is not a bad tree, but is in effect the same as a bad tree!—The fig is not a good tree, but is in effect the same as a good tree!—The Diatribe is not, indeed, impious, but says and does nothing but what is impious!

IT has happened to these assertors of "Freewill" according to the old proverb, 'Striving dire Scylla's rock to shun, they 'gainst Charybdis headlong run.' For devotedly striving to dissent from the Pelagians, they begin to deny the 'merit of worthiness;' whereas, by the very way in which they deny it, they establish it more firmly than ever. They deny it by their word and pen, but establish it in reality, and in heart-sentiment: and thus, they are worse than the Pelagians themselves: and that, on two accounts. First, the Pelagians plainly, candidly, and ingenuously, assert the 'merit of worthiness;' thus calling a boat a boat, and a fig a fig; and teaching what they really think. Whereas, our "Freewill" friends, while they think and teach the same thing, yet mock us with lying words and false appearances, as though they dissented from the Pelagians; when the fact is quite the contrary. So that, with respect to their hypocrisy, they seem to be the Pelagians' strongest opposers, but with respect to the reality of the matter, and their heart-tenet, they are twice-dipped Pelagians. And next, under this hypocrisy, they estimate and purchase the grace of God at a much lower rate than the Pelagians themselves. For these assert that it is not a certain little something in us by which we attain unto grace, but whole, full, perfect, great, and many, devoted efforts and works. Whereas, our friends declare, that it is a certain little something, almost a nothing, by which we deserve grace.

If therefore there must be error, they err with more honesty and less pride, who say, that the grace of God is purchased at a great price, and who account it dear and precious, than those who teach that it may be purchased at that which is very little and inconsiderable, and who account it cheap and contemptible. But however, Paul pounds both in pieces in one mortar, by one word, where he says that all are "justified freely;" and again that they are justified "without the Law" and "without the works of the Law." And he who asserts that the justification must be free in all who are justified, leaves none excepted who work, deserve, or prepare themselves; he leaves no work which can be called 'merit of congruity' or 'merit of worthiness;' and by the one hurling of this thunderbolt, he dashes in pieces both the Pelagians with their 'whole merit,' and the Sophists with their 'very little merit.' For a free justification allows of no workmen: because a free gift and a work-preparation are manifestly in opposition to each other.

Moreover, the act of being justified through grace will not allow of respect unto the worthiness of any person: as the apostle says also afterwards, chap. 11, "If by grace then it is no more of works: otherwise, grace is no more grace." (Rom. 11:6). He says the same also, "Now to him that worketh, is the reward not reckoned of grace, but of debt." (Rom. 4:4). Wherefore, my Paul stands an invincible destroyer of "Freewill," and lays prostrate two armies by one word. For if we be justified "without works," all works are condemned, whether they be very little, or very great. He excepts none, but thunders alike against all.

HERE you may see the yawning inconsiderateness of all our friends, and what it profits a man to rely upon the ancient church fathers, who have been approved down through so many ages. Were they not also all alike blind to, nay rather, did they not disregard, the most clear and most manifest words of Paul? Pray what is there that can be spoken clearly and plainly in defense of grace, against "Freewill," if the argument of Paul be not clear and plain? He proceeds with a glow of argument, and exalts grace against works; and that, in words the most clear and most plain; saying, that we are "justified freely," and that grace is no more grace, if it be sought by works. Thus most manifestly excluding all works in the matter of justification, to the intent that he might establish grace only, and free justification. And yet we, in all this light, still seek after darkness; and when we cannot ascribe unto ourselves great things, and all things, we endeavour to ascribe unto ourselves a something 'in degree,' 'a very little;' merely that we might maintain our tenet, that justification through the grace of God is not "free" and "without works."—As though he who declares, that greater things, and all things profit us nothing unto justification, does not much more deny that things 'in degree,' and things 'very little,' profit us nothing also: particularly when he has settled the point, that we are justified by grace alone without any works whatever, and therefore, without the Law itself, in which are comprehended all works, great and small, works of 'congruity' and works of 'worthiness.'

Go now then and boast of the authorities of the ancients, and depend on what they say; all of whom you see, to a man, disregarded Paul, that most plain and most clear teacher; and, as it were, purposely shunned this morning star, yea, this sun rather, because, being wrapped up in their own carnal reason, they thought it absurd that no place should be left to merit.

LET us now bring forward that example of Abraham which Paul afterwards quotes. "If (says he) Abraham were justified by works, he hath whereof to glory, but not before God. For what says the Scripture? Abraham believed God, and it was counted unto him for righteousness." (Rom. 4:2-3).

Mark here again, I pray you, the distinction of Paul, where he is showing the double righteousness of Abraham.—The one, is of works; that is, moral and civil; but he denies that he was justified by this before God, even though he were justified by it before men. Moreover, by that righteousness, "he hath whereof to glory" before men, but is all the while himself without the glory of God. Nor can anyone here say, that they are the works of the Law, or of ceremonies, which are here condemned; seeing that Abraham lived so many years before the Law. Paul plainly speaks of the works of Abraham, and those his *best works*. For it would be ridiculous to dispute, whether or not anyone were justified by *evil works*.

If therefore, Abraham be righteous by no works whatever, and if both he himself and all his works be left under sin, unless he be clothed with another righteousness, even with the righteousness of faith, it is quite manifest, that no man can do anything by works towards his becoming righteous: and moreover, that no works, no devoted efforts, no endeavours of "Freewill," avail anything in the sight of God, but are all judged to be ungodly, unrighteous, and evil. For if the man himself be not righteous, neither will his works or endeavours be righteous: and if they be not righteous, they are damnable, and merit wrath.

The other righteousness is that of faith; which consists, not in any works, but in the favor and imputation of God through grace. And mark how Paul dwells upon the word "imputed;" how he urges it, repeats it, and inculcates it.—"Now (says he) to him that worketh, is the reward not reckoned of grace, but of debt. But to him that worketh not, but believeth in Him that justifieth the ungodly, his faith is counted for righteousness," (Rom. 4:4-5), according to the purpose of the grace of God. Then he brings forth David, saying the same thing concerning the imputation through grace. "Blessed is the man to whom the Lord will not impute sin, . . ." (Rom. 4:6-8).

In this chapter, he repeats the word "impute" more than ten times. In a word, he distinctively sets forth "him that works," and "him that works not," leaving no *middle ground* between them. He declares, that righteousness is not imputed "to him that works," but asserts that righteousness is imputed "to him that works not," *if he believe*! Here is no way by which "Freewill," with its devoted efforts and endeavours, can escape or get off: it must be numbered with "him that works," or with "him that works not." If it be numbered with "him that works," you hear that righteousness is not imputed unto it; if it be numbered with "him that works not, but believes" in God, righteousness is imputed unto it. And then, it will not be the power of "Freewill," but the new creature by faith. But if righteousness be not imputed unto it, being "him that works," then, it becomes manifest, that all its works are nothing but sins, evils, and impieties before God.

Nor can any Sophist here snarl, and say, that, although *man* be evil, yet his *work* may not be evil. For Paul speaks not of the man simply, but of "him that works," to the very intent that he might declare in the plainest words, that the works and devoted efforts themselves of man are condemned, whatever they may be, by whatever name they may be called, or under whatever form they may be done. He here also speaks of good works; because the points of his argument are justification and merits. And when he speaks of "him that works," he speaks of all workers and of all their works; but more especially of their good and meritorious works. Otherwise, his distinction between "him that works," and "him that works not," will amount to nothing.

I HERE omit to bring forward those all-powerful arguments drawn from the purpose of grace, from the promise, from the force of the Law, from original sin, and from the election of God; of which, there is not one that would not of itself utterly overthrow "Freewill." For if grace comes by the purpose of God, or by election, it comes of necessity, and not by any devoted effort or endeavour of our own; as I have already shown. Moreover, if God promised grace before the Law, as Paul argues here, and in his epistle to the Galatians also, then it does not come by works or by the Law; otherwise, it would be no longer a *promise*. And so also faith, if works were of any avail, would come to nothing: by which, nevertheless, Abraham was justified before the Law was given. Again, as the Law is the strength of sin, and only makes sin obvious, but does not take it away, it convicts the conscience as guilty before God. This is what Paul means when he says, "the Law worketh wrath." (Rom. 4:15). How then can it be possible, that righteousness should be obtained by the Law? And if we derive no help from the Law, how can we derive any help from the power of "Freewill" alone?

Moreover, since we all lie under the same sin and damnation of the one man Adam, how can we attempt anything which is not sin and damnable? For when he says "all," he excepts no one; neither the power of "Freewill," nor any workman; whether he work or work not, attempt or attempt not, he must of necessity be included among the rest in the "all." Nor should we sin or be damned by that one sin of Adam, if the sin were not our own: for who could be damned for the sin of another, especially in the sight of God? Nor is the sin ours by imitation, or by working; for this would not be the one sin of Adam; because, then, it would not be the sin which he committed, but which we committed ourselves;—it becomes our sin by generation.—But of this in some other place.—Original sin itself, therefore, will not allow of any other power in "Freewill," but that of sinning and going on unto damnation. [101]

93. BUT however, before we hear the Evangelist John, I will just add the crowning testimony from Paul: and I am prepared, if this be not

sufficient, to oppose Paul to "Freewill" by commenting upon him throughout. Where he divides the human race into two distinctive divisions, "flesh" and "spirit," he speaks thus—"They that are after the flesh, do mind the things of the flesh; but they that are after the Spirit, do mind the things of the Spirit," (Rom. 8:5). As Christ also does, "That which is born of the flesh is flesh; and that which is born of the Spirit is spirit," (John 3:6).

That Paul here calls all carnal who are not spiritual, is manifest, both from the division itself and the opposition of spirit to flesh, and from the very words of Paul himself, where he adds, "But ye are not in the flesh but in the Spirit, if so be that the Spirit of God dwell in you. Now if any man have not the Spirit of Christ he is none of His" (Rom. 8:9). What else is the meaning of "But ye are not in the flesh, but in the Spirit, if so be that the Spirit of Christ dwell in you," but, that those who have not the "Spirit," are, necessarily, in the "flesh?" And if any man be not of Christ, what else is he but of Satan? It is manifest, therefore, that those who are devoid of the Spirit, are "in the flesh," and under Satan.

Now let us see what his opinion is concerning the endeavour and the power of "Freewill" in the carnal, who are in the flesh. "They cannot please God." Again, "The carnal mind is death." Again, "The carnal mind is enmity against God," And again,"It is not subject to the Law of God neither indeed can be." (Rom. 8:5-8). Here let the advocate for "Freewill" answer me—How can that endeavour toward good "which is death," which "cannot please God," which "is enmity *[that is, naturally hostile]* against God," which "is not subject to God," and "cannot" be subject to him? Nor does Paul mean to say, that the carnal mind is dead and hostile to God; but that, it is death itself, pure and unmitigated hostility itself which cannot possibly be subject to the Law of God or please God, as he had said just before, "For what the Law could not do, in that it was weak through the flesh, God did,". . . (Rom. 8:3).

But I am very well acquainted with that fable of Origen concerning the *triple affection*; the one of which he calls 'flesh,' the other 'soul,' and the other 'spirit,' making the soul that *middle ground* affection, free to choose either way, towards the flesh or towards the spirit. But these are merely his own dreams; he speaks them forth only, but does not prove them. Paul here calls every thing "flesh" that is without the "Spirit," as I have already shown. Therefore, those most exalted virtues of the best men are in the flesh; that is, they are dead, and with deep hostility toward God; they are not subject to the Law of God, nor indeed can be; and they please not God. For Paul does not only say that such men *are not* subject, but that they *cannot* be subject. So also Christ says, "An evil tree cannot bring forth good fruit." (Matt. 7:17). And again, "How can ye being evil speak that which is good," (Matt. 12:34). Here you see, we not only speak that which is evil, but cannot speak that which is good.

And though He says in another place, that we who are evil know how to give good gifts unto our children, (Matt. 6:11), yet He denies that we do good, even when we give good gifts; because those good gifts which we give are the creatures of God; but we ourselves not being good, cannot give those good gifts well. For He is speaking unto all men; nay, even unto His own disciples. So that these two sentiments of Paul, that the just man lives "by faith," (Rom. 1:17), and that "whatsoever is not of faith is sin," (Rom. 14:23), stand confirmed: the latter of which follows from the former. For if there be nothing by which we are justified but faith only, it is evident that those who are not of faith, are not justified. And if they be not justified, they are sinners. And if they be sinners, they are evil trees and can do nothing but sin and bring forth evil fruit—Wherefore, "Freewill" is nothing but the servant of sin, of death, and of Satan, doing nothing, and being able to do or attempt nothing, but evil!

ADD to this that example, Rom. 10:24, taken out of Isaiah, "I was found of them that sought Me not, I was made manifest unto them that asked not for Me." He speaks this with reference to the Gentiles:—that it was given unto them to hear and know Christ, when before, they could not even think of Him, much less seek Him, or prepare themselves for Him by the power of "Freewill." From this example it is sufficiently evident, that grace comes so free, that no thought concerning it, or attempt or desire after it, precedes. So also Paul—when he was Saul, what did he do by that exalted power of "Freewill?" Certainly, in respect of reason, he intended that which was best and most meritoriously good. But by what endeavours did he come unto grace? He did not only not seek after it, but received it even when he was furiously maddened against it!

On the other hand, he says of the Jews "The Gentiles which followed not after righteousness have attained unto the righteousness which is of faith. But Israel which followed after the Law of righteousness hath not attained unto the Law of righteousness" (Rom. 9:30-31). What has any advocate for "Freewill" to mutter against this? The Gentiles when filled with ungodliness and every vice, receive righteousness freely from a mercy-showing God: while the Jews, who follow after righteousness with all their devoted effort and endeavour, are frustrated. Is this not plainly saying, that the endeavour of "Freewill" is all in vain, even when it strives to do the best; and that "Freewill," of itself, can only fall back and grow worse and worse?

Nor can anyone say that the Jews did not follow after righteousness with all the power of "Freewill." For Paul himself bears this testimony of them, "That they had a zeal of God but not according to knowledge," (Rom. 10:2). Therefore, nothing which is attributed to "Freewill" was lacking to the Jews; and yet, it gained them nothing, nay to the contrary of that after which they strove *[they were rejected by God]*. Whereas, there was nothing in the Gentiles which is attributed to "Freewill," and they attained unto the righteousness of God *[with no apparent merit or effort on their part]*. And what is this but a most manifest example from each nation, and a most clear testimony of Paul, proving that grace is

---

given freely to the most undeserving and unworthy, and is not attained unto by any devoted efforts, endeavours, or works, either small or great, of any men, be they the best and most meritorious, or even of those who have sought and followed after righteousness with all the ardour of zeal? [102]

Luther cries out to St. Anne in the lightning storm. Luther's friend, Alexis, is killed by a flash of lightning close beside him, on a journey, when they were traveling together. "At the end of the year 1505 (says Mathesius) a dear friend of Luther's having been killed, and he himself having been much frightened by a tremendous thunderstorm, which terrified him with the thought of God's anger, and of the Last Judgment, he resolved in his own mind, and made a vow, that he would go into a convent, where he would serve God, and appease Him by saying masses, and gain eternal happiness by monastic sanctity." The artist, for his purpose has combined the two incidents, as though the friend had been killed by a thunderbolt.

Source: *The Life of Luther in Forty-Eight Historical Engravings* by Gustav Koenig, as published by the Engberg-Holmberg Publishing Co. of Chicago. The edition is undated, but appears to be from the late 19th century or very early 20th century. Courtesy of the Archives of the Evangelical Lutheran Church in America.

CHAPTER 22:

THE APOSTLE JOHN'S TESTIMONY

> People become God's sons only by being born of God — that is, an act of God's sovereign will. The false doctrine of the free will of man always accompanies the false doctrine of salvation by some kind of merit on man's part. No man comes to Christ unless the Father draws him. Period.

94. NOW let us come to JOHN, who is also a most copious and powerful subverter of "Freewill."

He, at the very first outset, attributes to "Freewill" such blindness, that it cannot even see the light of the truth: so far is it from possibility, that it should endeavour after it. He speaks thus, "The light shineth in darkness, and the darkness comprehended it not." (John 1:5). And directly afterwards, "He was in the world, and the world knew Him not; He came unto His own, and His own knew Him not." (Verses 1011).

What do you imagine he means by "world?" Will you attempt to separate any man from being included in this term, but him who is born again of the Holy Spirit? The term "world" is very particularly used by this apostle; by which he means, the whole race of men. Whatever, therefore, he says of the "world," is to be understood of the whole race of men. And hence, whatever he says of the "world," is to be understood also of "Freewill," as that which is most excellent in man. According to this apostle, then, the "world" does not know the light of truth; the "world" hates Christ and His followers; the "world" neither knows nor sees the Holy Spirit; the whole "world" is settled in everlasting hostility toward God; all that is in the "world," is "the lust of the flesh, the lust of the eyes, and the pride of life." "Love not the world." "Ye (says He)

are not of the world." "The world cannot hate you; but Me it hateth, because I testify of it that the works thereof are evil."

All these and many other like passages are proclamations of what "Freewill' is—'the principal part' of the world, ruling the empire of Satan! For John also himself speaks of the world by antithesis; making the "world" to be everything in the world which is not translated into the kingdom of the Spirit. So also Christ says to the apostles, "I have chosen you out of the world, and ordained you . . ." (John 15:16). If therefore, there were any in the world, who, by the powers of "Freewill" endeavoured so as to attain unto good, (which would be the case if "Freewill" could do any thing) John certainly ought, in reverence for these persons, to have softened down the term, lest, by a word of such general application, he should involve them in all those evils of which he condemns the world. But as he does not do this, it is evident that he makes "Freewill" guilty of all that is laid to the charge of the world: because, whatever the world does, it does by the power of "Freewill": that is, by its will and by its reason, which are its most exalted faculties.—He then goes on,

"But as many as received Him, to them gave He power to become the sons of God; even to them that believe on His Name, which were born, not of blood, nor of the will of the flesh, nor of the will of man, but of God." (John 1:12-13).

Having finished this distinctive division, he rejects from the kingdom of Christ, all that is "of blood," "of the will of the flesh," and "of the will of man." By "blood," I believe, he means the Jews; that is, those who wished to be the children of the kingdom, because they were the children of Abraham and of the Patriarchs; and hence, gloried in their "bloodline." By "the will of the flesh," I understand his meaning to be the devoted efforts of the people, which they exercised in the Law and in works: for "flesh" here signifies the carnal without the Spirit, who had indeed a will, and an endeavour, but who, because the Spirit was not in them, were carnal. By "the will of man," I understand he means the devoted efforts of all generally, that is, of the nations, or of any men whatever, whether exercised in the Law, or apart from the Law.

So that the sense is—they become the sons of God, neither by the birth of the flesh, nor by a devoted observance of the Law, nor by any devoted human effort whatever, but by a Divine birth only.

If therefore, they be neither born of the flesh, nor brought up by the Law, nor prepared by any human discipline, but are born again of God, it is manifest, that "Freewill" here profits nothing. For I understand "man," to signify here, according to the Hebrew manner of speech, *any man*, or *all men*; even as "flesh," is understood to signify, by antithesis, the people without the Spirit: and "the will of man," I understand to signify the greatest power in men, that is, that 'principal part,' "Freewill."

But be it so, that we do not dwell thus upon the signification of the words, singly; yet, the sum and substance of the meaning is most clear;—that John, by this distinctive division, rejects every thing that is not of Divine generation; since he says, that men are made the sons of God only by being born of God; which takes place, according to his own interpretation—*by believing on His name*! In this rejection therefore, "the will of man," or "Freewill," as it is not of divine generation, nor faith, is necessarily included. But if "Freewill" avail any thing, "the will of man" ought not to be rejected by John, nor ought men to be drawn away from it, and sent to faith and to the new birth only; lest that of Isaiah should be pronounced, against him, "Woe unto you that call good evil." Whereas now, since he rejects alike all "blood," "the will of the flesh," and "the will of man," it is evident, that "the will of man" avails nothing more towards making men the sons of God, than "blood" does, or the carnal birth. And no one doubts whether or not the carnal birth makes men the sons of God; for as Paul says, "They which are the children of the flesh, these are not the children of God;" (Rom. 9:8), which he proves by the examples of Ishmael and Esau.

THE same John, introduces John the Baptist speaking thus of Christ, "And of His fullness have all we received, and grace for grace." (John 1:16).

He says that grace is received by us out of the fullness of Christ—but for what merit or devoted effort? "For grace," says He; that is, of Christ; as Paul also says, "The grace of God, and the gift by grace, which is by one man Jesus Christ, hath abounded unto many." (Rom. 5:15).—Where is now the endeavour of "Freewill" by which grace is obtained! John and Paul here say, that grace is not only not received for any devoted effort of our own, but even *[and actually]* for the grace of another, or the merit of another, that is "of one Man Jesus Christ." Therefore, it is either false that we receive our grace for the grace of another, or else it is evident that "Freewill" is nothing at all; for both cannot consist—that the grace of God is both so cheap that it may be obtained in common and everywhere by the 'little endeavour' of any man; and at the same time so dear, that it is given unto us only in and through the grace of one Man, and He so great!

And I would also, that the advocates for "Freewill" be admonished in this place, that when they assert "Freewill," they are deniers of Christ. For if I obtain grace by my own endeavours, what need have I of the grace of Christ for the receiving of my grace? Or, what do I lack when I have gotten the grace of God? For the Diatribe has said, and all the Sophists say, that we obtain grace, and are prepared for the reception of it, by our own endeavours; not however according to 'worthiness,' but according to 'congruity.' This is plainly denying Christ: for whose grace, John the Baptist here testifies, that we receive grace. For as to that contrivance about 'worthiness' and 'congruity,' I have refuted that already, and proved it to be a mere play upon empty words, while the 'merit of worthiness' is really intended; and that, to a more impious length than ever the Pelagians themselves went, as I have already shown. And hence, the ungodly Sophists, together with the Diatribe, have more atrociously denied the Lord Christ who bought us, than ever the Pelagians, or any heretics have denied Him. So far is it from possibility, that grace should allow of any particle or power of "Freewill!"

But however, that the advocates for "Freewill" deny Christ, is proved, not by this Scripture only, but by their own very way of life. For by their "Freewill," they have made Christ to be unto them no longer a sweet Mediator, but a dreaded Judge, whom they strive to please by the intercessions of the Virgin Mother, and of the Saints; and also, by variously invented works, by rites, ordinances, and vows; by all of which, they aim at appeasing Christ, in order that He might give them grace. But they do not believe that He intercedes before God and obtains grace for them by His blood and grace; as it is here said, "for grace." And as they believe, so it is unto them! For Christ is in truth, an inexorable judge to them, and justly so; for they leave Him, who is a Mediator and most merciful Saviour, and account His blood and grace of less value than the devoted efforts and endeavours of their "Freewill!"

Now let us hear an example of "Freewill."—Nicodemus is a man in whom there is every thing that you can desire which "Freewill" is able to do. For what does that man omit either of devoted effort, or endeavour? He confesses Christ to be true, and to have come from God; he declares His miracles; he comes by night to hear Him, and to converse with Him. Does he not appear to have sought after, by the power of "Freewill," those things which pertain unto piety and salvation? But mark what shipwreck he makes. When he hears the true way of salvation by a new birth to be taught by Christ, does he acknowledge it, or confess that he had ever sought after it? Nay, he revolts from it, and is confounded; so much so, that he does not only say he does not understand it, but raises an objection against it—"How (says he) can these things be?" (John 3:9).

And no wonder: for whoever heard that man must be born again unto salvation "of water and of the Spirit?" (5). Whoever thought that the Son of God must be exalted, "that whosoever should believe in Him should not perish but have everlasting life?" (15). Did the greatest and most acute philosophers ever make mention of this? Did the princes of this world ever possess this knowledge? Did the "Freewill" of any man ever attain unto this by endeavours? Does not Paul confess it to be "wisdom hidden in a mystery," foretold indeed by the Prophets, but revealed by the Gospel? So that, it was secret and hidden from the world.

In a word: Ask experience: and the whole world, human reason itself, and in consequence, "Freewill" itself is compelled to confess, that it never knew Christ, nor heard of Him, before the Gospel came into the world. And if it did not know Him, much less could it seek after Him, search for Him, or endeavour to come unto Him. But Christ is "the way" of truth, life, and salvation. It must confess, therefore, whether it will or no, that, of its own powers, it neither knew nor could seek after those things which pertain unto the way of truth and salvation. And yet, contrary to this our own very confession and experience, like madmen we dispute in empty words, that there is in us that power remaining, which can both know and apply itself unto those things which pertain unto salvation! This is nothing more or less than saying, that Christ the Son of God was exalted for us, when no one could ever have known it or thought of it; but that, nevertheless, this very ignorance is not an ignorance, but a knowledge of Christ; that is, of those things which pertain unto salvation.

Do you not yet then see and palpably feel out, that the assertors of "Freewill" are plainly mad, while they call that knowledge, which they themselves confess to be ignorance? Is this not to "put darkness for light?" (Isaiah 5:20). But so it is, though God so powerfully stop the mouth of "Freewill" by its own confession and experience, yet even then, it cannot keep silence and give God the glory.

AND now farther, as Christ is said to be "the way, the truth, and the life," (John 14:6), and that, by positive assertion, so that whatever is not Christ is not the way but error, is not the truth but a lie, is not the life but death, it of necessity follows, that "Freewill," as it is neither Christ nor in Christ, must be bound in error, in a lie, and in death. Where now will be found that middle ground and neutral place—that the power of "Freewill," which is not in Christ, that is, in the way, the truth, and the life, is yet not of necessity either error, or a lie, or death?

For if all things which are said concerning Christ and grace were not said by positive assertion, that they might be opposed to anything and everything to the contrary; that is, that outside of Christ there is nothing but Satan, outside of grace nothing but wrath, outside of the light nothing but darkness, outside of the life nothing but death—what, I ask you, would be the use of all the Writings of the Apostles, nay, of the whole Scripture? The whole would be written in vain; because, they would not fix the point, that Christ is necessary (which, nevertheless, is their especial design) and for this reason,—because a middle, neutral position would be discovered, which of itself, would be neither evil nor good, neither of Christ nor of Satan, neither true nor false, neither alive nor dead, and perhaps, neither anything nor nothing; and that would be called, 'that which is most excellent and most exalted' in the whole race of men!

Take it therefore whichever way you will.—If you grant that the Scriptures speak in positive assertion, you can say nothing for "Freewill," but that which is contrary to Christ: that is, you will say that error, death, Satan, and all evils reign in Him. If you do not grant that they speak in positive assertion, you weaken the Scriptures, make them to establish nothing, not even to prove that Christ is necessary. And thus, while you establish "Freewill," you make Christ void, and bring the whole Scripture to destruction. And though you may pretend, verbally, that you confess Christ; yet, in reality and in heart, you deny Him. For if the power of "Freewill" be not a thing erroneous altogether, and damnable, but sees and wills those things which are good and meritorious, and which pertain unto salvation, it is whole, it wants not the physician Christ, nor does Christ redeem that part of man.—For what need is there for light and life, where there is light and life already?

Moreover, if that power be not redeemed, the best part in man is not redeemed, but is of itself good and whole. And then also, God is unjust if He damn any man; because, He damns that which is the most excellent in man, and whole; that is, He damns him when innocent. For there is no man who has not "Freewill." And although the evil man abuse this, yet this power itself, (according to what you teach) is not so destroyed, but that it can and does endeavour towards good. And if it be such, it is without doubt good, holy, and just: wherefore, it ought not to be damned, but to be distinctly separated from the man who is to be damned. But this cannot be done, and even if it could be done, man would then be without "Freewill," nay, he would not be man at all, he would neither have merit nor demerit, he could neither be damned nor saved, but would be completely a brute, and no longer immortal. It follows therefore, that God is unjust who damns that good, just, and holy power, which, though it be in an evil man, does not need Christ as the evil man does.

BUT let us proceed with John. "He that believeth on Him, (says he) is not condemned; but he that believeth not is condemned already, because he hath not believed on the Name of the only begotten Son of God. (John 3:18).

Tell me!—Is "Freewill" included in the number of those that believe, or not? If it be so, then again, it has no need of grace; because, of itself, it believes on Christ—whom, of itself it never knew nor thought of! If it be not, then it is judged already and what is this but saying, that it is damned in the sight of God? But God damns none but the ungodly: therefore, it is ungodly. And what godliness can that which is ungodly endeavour after? For I do not think that the power of "Freewill" can be excepted; seeing that, he speaks of the whole man as being condemned.

Moreover, unbelief is not one of the grosser affections, but is that chief affection seated and ruling on the throne of the will and reason; just the same as its contrary, faith. For to be unbelieving, is to deny God, and to make him a liar; "If we believe not we make God a liar," (1 John 5:10). How then can that power, which is contrary to God, and which makes Him a liar, endeavour after that which is good? And if that power be not unbelieving and ungodly, John ought not to say of the *whole man* that he is condemned already, but to speak thus,—Man, according to his 'grosser affections,' is condemned already; but according to that which is best and 'most excellent,' he is not condemned; because, that endeavours after faith, or rather, is already believing.

Hence, where the Scripture so often says, "All men are liars," we must, upon the authority of "Freewill," on the contrary say—the Scripture rather, lies; because, man is not a liar as to his *best part*, that is, his reason and will, but as to his *flesh* only, that is, his blood and his grosser part: so that that *whole,* according to which he is called man, that is, his reason and his will, is sound and holy. Again, there is that word of John the Baptist, "He that believeth on the Son hath everlasting life; he that believeth not the Son shall not see life, but the wrath of God abideth on him." (John 3:36). We must understand "upon him" thus:—that is, the wrath of God abides upon the 'grosser affections' of the man: but upon that power of "Freewill," that is, upon his will and his reason, abide grace and everlasting life.

Hence, according to this, in order that "Freewill" might stand, whatever is in the Scriptures said against the ungodly, you are, by a sort of verbal sleight of hand, to twist around to apply to that brute part of

---

man, that the truly rational and human part might remain safe. I have therefore, to render thanks to the assertors of "Freewill;" because, I may sin with all confidence; knowing that my reason and will or my "Freewill" cannot be damned, because it cannot be destroyed by my sinning, but forever remains sound, righteous, and holy. And thus, happy in my will and reason, I shall rejoice that my filthy and brute flesh is distinctly separated from me, and damned; so far shall I be from wishing Christ to become its Redeemer!—You see, here, to what the doctrine of "Freewill" brings us—it denies all things, divine and human, temporal and eternal; and with all these enormities makes a laughing-stock of itself!

AGAIN, the Baptist says, "A man can receive nothing, except it were given him from above." (John 3:27).

Let not the Diatribe here produce its forces, where it enumerates all those things which we have received from heaven. We are now disputing, not about nature, but about grace: we are inquiring, not what we are upon earth, but what we are in heaven before God.

> We know that man was constituted lord over those things which are beneath himself; over which, he has a right and a Freewill, that those things might do, and obey as he wills and thinks. But we are now inquiring whether he has a "Freewill" over God, that He should do and obey in those things which man wills: or rather, whether God has not a Freewill over man, that he should will and do what God wills, and should be able to do nothing but what He wills and does.

John the Baptist here says, that he "can receive nothing, except it be given him from above."—Wherefore, "Freewill" must be a nothing at all!

Again, "He that is of the earth, is earthly and speaketh of the earth, He that cometh from heaven is above all." (John 3:31).

Here again, he makes all those earthly, who are not of Christ, and says that they savour and speak of earthly things only, nor does he leave anyone on a middle ground. But surely, "Freewill" is not "He that cometh from heaven." Wherefore it must of necessity, be "he that is of the earth," and that speaks of the earth and savours of the earth. But if there were any power in man, which at any time, in any place, or by any work, did not savour of the earth, the Baptist ought to have excepted this person, and not to have said in a general way concerning all those who are out of Christ, that they are of the earth, and speak of the earth.

So also afterwards, Christ says, "Ye are of the world, I am not of the world. Ye are from beneath, I am from above." (John 8:23).

And yet, those to whom He spoke had "Freewill," that is, reason and will; but still He says, that they are "of the world." But what news would He have given them, if He had merely said, that they were of the world, as to their 'grosser affections?' Did not the whole world know this before? Moreover, what need was there for His saying that men were of the world, as to that part in which they are mere mortal beings? For according to that, animals are also of the world.

AND now what do those words of Christ, where He says, "No one can come unto Me except My Father which hath sent Me draw [1] him," (John 6:44), leave to "Freewill?"

For He says it is necessary, that every one should hear and learn of the Father Himself, and that all must be "taught of God." Here, indeed, He not only declares that the works and devoted efforts of "Freewill" are of no avail, but that even the word of the Gospel itself, (of which He is here speaking,) is heard in vain, unless the Father Himself speak

---

[1]

Understanding the Greek word **helkúō** translated *draw* is very helpful. The Greek tense is aorist subjunctive active. Strong's number 1670. Review Acts 16:19; 21:30; James 2:6; John 12:32; 18:10 John 21:6,11 where the same Greek word is used. As people are actively compelling someone in these passages, so God is active in His *compelling,* but *not* forcing against the will, of His elect to come to Christ. Drawing by God is not simply wooing or inviting, but is *effective* in that those who are drawn are *inwardly* compelled to follow. No one who is drawn by God in this manner chooses not to follow.

within, and teach and draw. "No one can," "No one can (says He) come:" by which, that power, whereby man can endeavour something towards Christ, that is, towards those things which pertain unto salvation, is declared to be a nothing at all.

Nor does that at all profit "Freewill," which the Diatribe brings forward out of Augustine, by way of casting a slur upon this all-clear and all-powerful Scripture—'that God draws us, in the same way as we draw a sheep, by holding out to it a green bough.' By this example he would prove that there is in us *a power to follow the drawing of God*. But this example avails nothing in the present passage. For God holds out, not one of His good things only, but many, nay, even His Son, Christ Himself; and yet no man follows Christ, *unless* the Father draws the person in a special manner through a spiritual work done within, and supernaturally, by His Spirit!—Nay, *[without the special drawing of God]* the whole world persecutes the Son whom He holds forth!

But this illustration harmonizes sweetly with the experience of the godly, who are now made sheep, and know God their Shepherd. These, living in, and being moved by, the Spirit, follow wherever God wills, and whatever He shows them. But the ungodly man comes not unto Him, even when he hears the Word, unless the Father draw and teach within: which He does by shedding abroad His Spirit. And where that is done, there is a different kind of drawing from that which is external: there, Christ is held forth in the illumination of the Spirit, whereby the man is drawn unto Christ with the sweetest of all drawing: under which, he is passive while God speaks, teaches, and draws, rather than seeks or runs of himself.

I WILL produce yet one more passage from John, where, he says, "The Spirit shall reprove the world of sin, because they believe not in me." (John 16:9).

You here see that it is sin not to believe in Christ: And this sin is seated, not in the skin, nor in the hairs of the head, but in the very reason and will. Moreover, as Christ makes the whole world guilty from this sin, and as it is known by experience that the world is ignorant of this sin, as much so as it is ignorant of Christ, seeing that, it must be *revealed* by the *reproof* of the Spirit; it is manifest, that "Freewill," together with its will and reason, is accounted a captive of this sin, and condemned before God. Wherefore, as long as it is ignorant of Christ and believes not in Him, it can will or attempt nothing good, but necessarily serves that sin of which it is ignorant.

In a word: Since the Scripture declares Christ everywhere by positive assertion and by antithesis, (as I said before), in order that, it might subject every thing that is without the Spirit of Christ, to Satan, to ungodliness, to error, to darkness, to sin, to death, and to the wrath of God, all the testimonies concerning Christ must make directly against "Freewill;" and they are innumerable, nay, the whole of the Scripture. If therefore our subject of discussion is to be decided by the judgment of the Scripture, the victory, in every respect, is mine; for there is not one jot or tittle of the Scripture remaining, which does not condemn the doctrine of "Freewill" altogether! But if the great theologians and defenders of "Freewill" know not, or pretend not to know, that the Scripture every where declares Christ by positive assertion and by antithesis, yet all Christians know it, and in common confess it. They know, I say, that there are two kingdoms in the world mutually militating against each other.—That Satan reigns in the one, who, on that account is by Christ called "the prince of this world," (John 12:31), and by Paul "the God of this world;" (2 Cor. 4:4), who, according to the testimony of the same Paul, holds all persons captive according to his will, who are not rescued from him by the Spirit of Christ: nor does he allow any to be rescued by any other power but that of the Spirit of God: as Christ testifies in the parable of "the strong man armed" keeping his palace in peace.—In the other kingdom Christ reigns: which kingdom, continually resists and wars against that of Satan: into which we are translated, not by any power of our own, but by the grace of God, whereby we are delivered from this present evil world, and are snatched from the power of darkness. The knowledge and confession of these two kingdoms, which thus ever mutually fight against each other with so much power and force, would alone be sufficient to disprove the doctrine of "Freewill:" seeing that, we are compelled to serve in the kingdom of Satan, until we are liberated by a Divine Power. All this, I say, is known in common among Christians, and fully confessed in their proverbs, by their prayers, by their pursuits, and by their whole lives.

I OMIT to bring forward that truly Achillean Scripture of mine, which the Diatribe proudly passes by untouched—I mean, that which Paul teaches, Rom. 7 and Gal. 5, that there is in the saints, and in the godly, so powerful a warfare between the spirit and the flesh, that they cannot do what they would.

> From this warfare I argue thus:—If the nature of man be so evil, even in those who are born again of the Spirit, that it does not only not endeavour after good, but is even opposed to, and militates against good, how should it endeavour after good in those who are not born again of the Spirit, and who are still in the "old man," and serve under Satan?

Nor does Paul there speak of the 'grosser affections' only, (by means of which, as a common impersonator, the Diatribe is accustomed to get out of the way of all the Scriptures,) but he enumerates among the works of the flesh heresy, idolatry, contentions, divisions, etcetera; which he describes as reigning in those most exalted faculties; that is, in the reason and the will. If therefore, flesh with these affections war against the Spirit in the saints, much more will it war against God in the ungodly, and in "Freewill." Hence, Rom. 8:7, he calls it "enmity against God."—I should like, I say, to see this argument of mine overturned, and "Freewill" defended against it. [103]

CHAPTER 23:

LUTHER'S PERSONAL TESTIMONY AGAINST FREE WILL

Luther recalls his own despair, which resulted in his finding the grace of God. Salvation by works always leaves one in doubt of his salvation. God has taken Luther's salvation out of Luther's hands and has given him great confidence and assurance.

95. As to myself, I openly confess, that I should not wish "Freewill" to be granted me, even if it could be so, nor anything else to be left in my own hands, whereby I might endeavour something towards my own salvation. And that, not merely because in so many opposing dangers, and so many assaulting devils, I could not stand and hold it fast, (in which state no man could be saved, seeing that one devil is stronger than all men;) but because, even though there were no dangers, no conflicts, no devils, I should be compelled to labor under a continual uncertainty, and to beat the air only. Nor would my conscience, even if I should live and work to all eternity, ever come to a settled certainty, how much it ought to do in order to satisfy God. For whatever work should be done, there would still remain a misgiving, whether or not it pleased God, or whether He required anything more; as is proved in the experience of all high-ranking judicial officers, and as I myself learned to my bitter cost, through so many years of my own experience.

But now, since God has put my salvation out of the way of *my* will, and has taken it under *His own*, and has promised to save me, not according to my working or manner of life, but according to His own grace and mercy, I rest fully assured and persuaded that He is faithful, and will not lie, and moreover great and powerful, so that no devils, no adversities can destroy Him, or pluck me out of His hand. "No one (says He) shall pluck

them out of My hand, because My Father which gave them Me is greater than all." (John 10:27-28). Hence it is certain, that in this way, if all are not saved, yet some, yea, many shall be saved; whereas by the power of "Freewill," no one could be saved, but all must perish together.

And moreover, we are certain and persuaded, that in this way, we please God, not from the merit of our own works, but from the favor of His mercy promised unto us; and that, if we work less, or work badly, He does not impute it unto us, but, as a Father, pardons us and makes us better.—This is the glorying which all the saints have in their God! [104]

Bruder Martin.

Luther as an Augustinian monk

CHAPTER 24:

A REVIEW OF GOD'S JUSTICE IN DAMNING THE UNGODLY

Human reason will never understand God's wisdom or justice in punishing the wicked. Who are we to judge the Almighty? There is a life after this life; and all that is not punished and repaid here will be punished and repaid there.

96. AND if you are concerned about this,—that it is difficult to defend the mercy and justice of God, seeing that He damns the undeserving, that is, those who are for that reason ungodly, because, being born in iniquity, they cannot by any means prevent themselves from being ungodly, and from remaining so, and being damned, but are compelled from the necessity of nature to sin and perish, as Paul says, "We all were the children of wrath, even as others," (Eph. 2:3.), when at the same time, they were created such by God Himself from a corrupt seed, by means of the sin of Adam,—

Here God is to be honoured and revered, as being most merciful towards those whom He justifies and saves in spite of all their unworthiness: and it is to be in no small degree ascribed unto His wisdom, that He causes us to believe Him to be just, even where He appears to be unjust. For if His righteousness were such, that it was considered to be righteousness according to human judgment, it would be no longer divine, nor would it in anything differ from human righteousness. But as He is the one and true God, and moreover incomprehensible and inaccessible by human reason, it is right, nay, it is necessary, that His righteousness should be incomprehensible: even as Paul exclaims, saying, "Oh the depth of the riches, both of the wisdom and knowledge of God, how unsearchable are His judgments,

---

and His ways past finding out!" (Rom. 11:33). But they would be no
longer "past finding out" if we were in all things able to see how they
were righteous. What is man, compared with God! What can our power
do, when compared with His power! What is our strength, compared
with His strength! What is our knowledge compared with His wisdom!
What is our substance, compared with His substance! In a word, what
is all that we are, compared with all that He is!

If then we confess, even according to the teaching of nature, that
human power, strength, wisdom, knowledge, substance, and all human
things together, are nothing when compared with the divine power,
strength, wisdom, knowledge, and substance, what perverseness must
it be in us to attack the righteousness and judgments of God only, and
to proudly credit so much to our own judgment, as to wish to
comprehend, judge, and rate the divine judgments! Why do we not,
here in like manner say at once—What! is our judgment nothing, when
compared with the divine judgments!—But ask reason herself if she is
not, from conviction, compelled to confess that she is foolish and rash
for not allowing the judgments of God to be incomprehensible, when she
confesses that all the other divine things are incomprehensible? In every
thing else we concede to God a Divine Majesty; and yet, are ready to
deny it to His judgments! Nor can we for a little while believe that He
is just, even when He promises that it shall come to pass, that when He
shall reveal His glory, we shall all see, and know with absolute certainty,
that He ever was, and is,—just!

BUT I will produce an example that may go to confirm this faith,
and to console that "evil eye" which suspects God of injustice.—Behold!
God so governs this physical world in external things, that, according
to human reason and judgment, you must be compelled to say, either
that there is no God, or that God is unjust: as a certain one says, 'I am
often tempted to think there is no God.' For see the great prosperity of
the wicked, and on the contrary the great adversity experienced by the

good; according to the testimony of the proverbs, and of Experience, the parent of all proverbs. The more abandoned men are, the more successful! "The tabernacles of robbers (says Job) prosper." And Psalm 73, complains, that the sinners of the world abound in riches. Is it not, I pray you, in the judgment of all, most unjust, that the evil should be prosperous, and the good afflicted? Yet so it is in the events of the world. And here it is, that the most exalted minds have so fallen, as to deny that there is any God at all; and to fable, that fortune disposes of all things at random: such were Epicurus and Pliny. And Aristotle, in order that he might make his 'First-cause Being' free from every kind of misery, is of the opinion that he thinks of nothing whatever but himself; because he considers, that it must be most irksome to him to see so many evils and so many injuries.

But the Prophets themselves, who believed there is a God, were tempted still more concerning the injustice of God, as Jeremiah, Job, David, Asaph, and others. And what do you suppose Demosthenes and Cicero thought, who, after they had done all they could, received no other reward than a miserable death? And yet all this, which is so very much like injustice in God, when set forth in those arguments which no reason or light of nature can resist, is most easily cleared up by the light of the Gospel, and the knowledge of grace: by which, we are taught, that the wicked flourish *in their bodies*, but lose *their souls*!

> And the whole of this unsolvable question is solved in one word—There is a life after this life: in which will be punished and repaid, everything that is not punished and repaid here: for this life is nothing more than an entrance on, and a beginning of, the life which is to come!

If then even the light of the Gospel, which stands in the Word and in the faith only, is able to effect so much as with ease to do away with, and settle this question which has been agitated through so many ages and never solved; how do you suppose matters will appear when the light of the Word and of faith shall cease, and the essential Truth itself shall be revealed in the Divine Majesty? Do you not suppose that the light of glory will then most easily solve that question, which is now unsolvable by the light of the Word and of grace, even as the light of grace now easily solves that question, which is unsolvable by the light of nature? [105]

Luther by Zimmerman

CHAPTER 25:

IN PRAISE OF GOD ALMIGHTY . . . .

Now unto the King eternal, immortal, invisible, the only wise God, be honour and glory for ever and ever. Amen. (1 Tim 1:17 KJV)

Luther points to and explains three lights: The light of nature, the light of grace, and the light of glory. These will one day all become focused upon the One true God and we will see clearly the absolute justice and righteousness of God.

97. Let us therefore hold in consideration the three lights—the light *of nature*, the light *of grace*, and the light *of glory*; which is the common, and a very good distinction. By the light of nature, it is unsolvable *how* it can be just, that the good man should be afflicted and the wicked should prosper: but this is solved by the light of grace. By the light of grace it is unsolvable, *how* God can damn him, who, by his own powers, can do nothing but sin and become guilty. Both the light of nature and the light of grace here say, that the fault is not in the miserable man, but in the unjust God: nor can they judge otherwise of that God, who crowns the wicked man freely without any merit, and yet crowns not, but damns another, who is perhaps less, or at least not more wicked. But the light of glory speaks otherwise.—That will show, that God, to whom alone belongs the judgment of incomprehensible righteousness, is of righteousness most perfect and most manifest; in order that we may, in the meantime, believe it, being admonished and confirmed by that example of the light of grace, which solves that which is as great a miracle to the light of nature!

---

98. I SHALL here draw this book to a conclusion: prepared if it were necessary to pursue this Discussion still farther. Though I consider that I have now abundantly satisfied the godly man, who wishes to believe the truth without making resistance. For if we believe it to be true, that God foreknows and foreordains all things; that He can be neither deceived nor hindered in His Foreknowledge and Predestination; and that nothing can take place but according to His Will, (which reason herself is compelled to confess;) then, even according to the testimony of Reason herself, there can be no "Freewill"—in man,—in angel,—or in any creature!

Hence:—If we believe that Satan is the prince of this world, ever ensnaring and fighting against the kingdom of Christ with all his powers; and that he does not let go of his captives without being forced by the Divine Power of the Spirit; it is manifest, that there can be no such thing as—"Freewill!"

Again:—If we believe that original sin has so destroyed us, that even in the godly who are led by the Spirit, it causes the utmost harassment by striving against that which is good; it is manifest, that there can be nothing left in a man devoid of the Spirit, which can turn itself towards good, but which must turn towards evil!

Again:—If the Jews, who followed after righteousness with all their powers, ran rather into unrighteousness, while the Gentiles who followed after unrighteousness attained unto a free righteousness which they never hoped for; it is equally manifest, from their very works, and from experience, that man, without grace, can do nothing but will evil!

Finally:—If we believe that Christ redeemed men by His blood, we are compelled to confess, that the whole man was lost: otherwise, we shall make Christ quite unnecessary, or a Redeemer of the grossest part of man only,—which is blasphemy and sacrilege! [106]

D^r. MART. LUTHER.

NINETY-FIVE THESES FOR THE
TWENTY-FIRST CENTURY CHURCH

Presented here for the reader's consideration are *Ninety-Five Theses for the Twenty-first Century Church* which the present author has derived (1) as a Bible student and believer in Jesus Christ, (2) during many years working in church volunteer ministry as a teacher and occasional preacher, (3) during a lengthy career in Christian school ministry as a teacher, administrator, disciplinarian of students and staff, counselor, and Bible teacher, and (4) as a result of studying Martin Luther's *Bondage* over a period of twenty years. Because these theses are not Scripture, the author remains willing to be shown any error contained therein.

1. Nearly all men everywhere believe they have free will. This includes a majority of those who profess to be believers in Jesus Christ. It is this great error within much of the church which prompted this present condensation of Martin Luther's book.

2. The false teaching and/or assumption that man has free will toward God, and that he can will himself into salvation by faith, and will himself out of salvation is a great error within much of the church. This is a second reason for this present work.

3. Just as the humanist Desiderius Erasmus argued against Luther in the distant past, the comparatively recent re-ascendence of secular humanism throughout western society — including the church — is the prime cause of the error in thought patterns and church doctrines today. It is this humanistic position which sits in judgment upon God's Word and refuses to agree with Martin Luther's biblical position regarding God's sovereignty and man's absolute inability to turn to God through an act of his own will.

4. One major purpose for preaching and teaching the gospel and all of its parts (that is, both Old and New Testaments, both Law and Grace) is that all who hear may know assuredly of their total guilt and utter helplessness before God---and that knowing their guilt they may call upon God to save them through Christ's atoning blood.

5. Those who name the name of Christ must cease and desist in saying or teaching that man has free will, since the Scriptures are quite clear — as proven conclusively from the Scriptures by Martin Luther — that man does not have free will toward God, or in any aspect of eternal salvation.

6. No one ever comes to God or seeks God by an act of his own will, though it may seem to be so. Man, by natural wisdom, has never sought God or found God, and such will never happen. The bondage of natural man's will is the reason that he cannot and will not seek after God.

7. The bondage of man's will to Satan and his helpless condition is a major theme of Scripture. For example, Israel in Egypt under Pharaoh's oppression (Exodus), and the lame man at the pool of Bethesda (John 5).

8. Man's sinful condition is so dreadful that none would be saved if it were not for the faithful preaching of the gospel by men and women of God and God's gifts of faith and grace to those whom He elected before the foundation of the world.

9. The person who has seriously contemplated and accepted the possibility of his ultimate and eternal rejection by God has better grounds to appreciate and comprehend the value of his eternal soul and God's grace in salvation.

10. If God did not elect, call, and justify *some*, none would be saved.

11. Although God foreknows, predestines, calls, justifies, and glorifies all who become saved, most are saved through the immediate instrumentality of the faithful preaching of the gospel.

12. While past history seems to indicate that only a few are saved by the direct intervention of God, in these last days there is significant evidence that God is intervening directly through dreams and visions revealing Himself directly to the lost, especially in Muslim nations. However, this in no way reduces or changes the Great Commission given by our Lord Jesus Christ.

13. Man's will is seldom, in man's consciousness, overruled by the will of God or by the work of His Holy Spirit in the sense of compelling a person to act against his own will. In other words, the work of God's Spirit always causes a person to change his mind so as to fulfil God's plan and foreknowledge.

14. While it may and often does seem to a person that he is, of his own free will, choosing to be saved, such can never be the case in the light of all Scripture taken together.

15. Man's will, whether a believer or an unbeliever, is always subject to God's omnipotent will and God's foreknowledge; therefore man's will is not completely free. Free will for man in relation to God is an illusion and is nowhere supported by Scripture.

16. Salvation, according to Scripture, is never a mental decision, but always a work of God in the heart, mind, will, and emotions.

17. Men only seek God and find God when, by God's wonderful mercy, they are drawn to God by His Holy Spirit.

18. Faith for salvation is a gift from God. Therefore, there is absolutely nothing in unregenerate man or no acts possible by unregenerate man, which can merit God's favor.

19. Salvation in Jesus Christ is by grace alone through faith alone. Both grace and faith are gifts of God. Only those to whom God gives faith will truly believe.

20. Salvation is never an act of one's own will. It is only God and His grace which brings salvation.

21. Absolutely nothing which a person does other than believing the gospel is an effective cause of one's new birth. Faith to believe the gospel is God's gift.

22. Salvation is always the result of an act of God's will — in eternity past when that person was elected to salvation, and in the present at the point in time when the elected person truly believes and receives Jesus Christ.

23. If a person does not and cannot will himself into salvation, it becomes clear that one cannot will himself out of salvation.

24. Those persons who appear to become believers and who later fall away and never return could not have been recipients of true salvation as is clear from many scriptures.

25. God is debtor to no man. Nothing done by man, including prayer, puts God in obligation to sinful man.

26. Repentance is a command of God to every living person (Acts 17:30). Many do not repent because (1) they have not heard the gospel, or (2) though hearing, they have not been given the gift to hear and believe.

27. The act of repentance, together with the outward evidences which follow, is commanded of all men (Acts 17:30), and is the outward evidence to the world and to the person repenting that God has given a new nature capable of obedience to God.

28. Though God has commanded all men everywhere to repent (Acts 17:30), only those to whom God grants faith will actually repent. (Acts 11:18)

29. Repentance is, in essence, somewhat equivalent to the new birth. They both are aspects of true salvation in Christ. They are each a special part of God's free gift of salvation.

30. The forgiveness of sin at the time of one's salvation is a once-and-for-all-time forgiveness of past, present, and future sins. It is a complete and total cleansing from all sin. Once cleansed, the true believer is forever clean in God's sight. It is just as Jesus said, "He who is bathed needs only to wash his feet, but is completely clean; and you are clean . . ." John 13:10 NKJV with 1 John 1:7

31. "Whosoever shall call upon the name of the Lord shall be saved." (Joel 2:32; Acts 2:21; Rom 10:13) Only those who are drawn to God by the Holy Spirit will truly call upon the Lord in the sense of this thrice-repeated promise of Scripture. (John 6:44,65)

32. If God foreknew and therefore elected a person before the foundation of the world, that person will receive the gifts of faith and grace and be saved in God's timing. (John 1:12; 3:16)

33. One's will is passive, but cooperative, in salvation. The new birth gives a person a new will which is not only capable, but willing to obey God.

34. The giving of a command by God does not assume or prove that men are capable of performing the command.

35. The giving of a command by God makes clear what men should do, what they ought to do, but does not prove that it is possible for men to do it.

36. God has given many commands which experience has proven and which is confirmed by scripture, that man has not carried out. For example, in at least two situations, after Jesus healed someone, He said to them "sin no more." (John 5:14; 8:11) This was and is an impossible command for humans, even if regenerated, to fully obey.

37. Scripture makes clear that the real reason God has made commands is so that man's complete inability to obey God's commands might become obvious and therefore man might be found guilty before God and in absolute need of a mighty Savior.

38. It is clear that God has revealed his general will throughout Scripture from Genesis to Revelation, and that God has also revealed the fact of his inscrutable will which is not fully explained.

39. There are many uses of the word "all" in Scripture which are often misinterpreted to mean every person on earth. However, *careful study of the context* uniformly reveals that often the word "all" refers to those persons whom God elected to be saved. One prime example is "The Lord is not slack concerning his promise, as some men count slackness; but is longsuffering to us-ward, not willing that any [of the elect] should perish, but that all [of the elect] should come to repentance. (2 Pet 3:9 KJV)

40. An incontrovertible fact of Jesus' teaching is that God's inscrutable will is that few will actually be saved, and most people will be lost. (Matt 7:14; 20:16; 22:14; Luke 13:23-30)

41. God's way of thinking — His reasoning, His justice, His choices regarding man and the creation — while not always understood by man now and in this life — are absolutely just and righteous because He always acts consistently with His holy and righteous and perfect nature.

42. A part of the faith God gives enables the believer to know that God is always absolutely just and good in the light of His Word and His holy nature.

43. Those who shall be saved were written in the Lamb's Book of Life from the foundation of the world. There is no scriptural proof that anyone's name was subsequently added to or subtracted from the Lamb's Book of Life.

44. God will be absolutely just to condemn all who go to hell. This is and will be true even though it may appear to us that some "good" persons will go there.

45. God will be absolutely just to take all to heaven who go there. This is and will be true even though it may appear to us that some "bad" persons go there.

46. In truth, it appears that God saves some people who are totally undeserving and God sends to hell some people who are totally undeserving. No one complains about God saving undeserving people, but many people always complain about God sending to hell people who are in man's opinion undeserving. By this paradox the believer should come to understand something of the fact that God's wisdom and justice are far above man's wisdom and justice.

47. God's absolute justice is intertwined with His mercy or no one would be saved.

48. In the only prayer of Jesus which God has permitted us to "overhear," He earnestly and repeatedly prayed for the unity of all believers. (John 17) Thus, it behooves all believers of every diverse doctrinal position to "[endeavor] to keep the unity of the Spirit in the bond of peace." (Eph 4:3 KJV)

49. The act of praying the "sinner's prayer" does not obligate God to save a person, nor does it necessitate the spiritual act of new birth.

50. The new birth is God's prerogative and no person may obligate or force God to do this work in a person's heart. Though a person may pray the sinner's prayer very sincerely, or numerous times, he may yet remain in an unsaved, unregenerate condition before God.

51. Nearly every child raised in a Bible-teaching church prays the sinner's prayer once or many times during childhood, but statistics tell us that only a small percentage stay true to their church's (and the Bible's) teachings as they mature into adulthood. This confirms that only a small percentage are truly born again as children.

52. Many have prayed the sinner's prayer, and not been saved or born again. These are dead works because they are not prompted by the Holy Spirit, and by true repentance which is also a gift of God.

53. Any personal worker, child evangelist, pastor, counselor, Sunday school teacher, Christian school teacher, etc. who gives assurance of salvation to someone who prays the sinner's prayer, or who considers that person saved as a result of praying the prayer is outside the bounds of Scriptural authority.

54. Just as the Catholic Church has held to the error that it can "dispense" salvation through the sacraments, and especially through baptism, in like manner many Protestants and evangelicals of the twentieth and twenty-first centuries have gained and held to the error that they can "dispense" salvation through the recitation of the sinner's prayer and/or water baptism.

55. A person can confess with his mouth that he is a sinner — such as is often done during the recitation of the sinner's prayer — without truly having experienced conviction for sin, or in fact believing in his heart that he is a lost sinner.

56. Because no one is saved as a result of reciting a prayer, it is a grievous sin against a person to tell him that he is saved because he has prayed the "sinner's prayer."

57. No person has the right or authority to give assurance of salvation to anyone.

58. No church, denomination, fellowship, or organization, has been given by God the authority to grant the assurance of salvation to any person. True spiritual assurance of eternal salvation is a work of the Holy Spirit as God-given faith takes hold of the promises of God in the Holy Scriptures.

59. Water baptism is not an instrumental cause of salvation, and completing the act of water baptism does not guarantee a person the assurance of salvation.

60. It is reserved strictly to the Holy Spirit through the Word of God to give a new believer true inner assurance of salvation, as well as to continue to give that assurance to the believer throughout his or her life.

61. Assurance of salvation in the believer's heart is a work of the Holy Spirit normally based upon repeated exposure to God's Word, the gift of faith from God, and the sovereign grace of God in opening the person's heart to believe and obey the gospel.

62. True assurance of salvation comes only as God gives a person faith to believe, as faith takes hold of the Word of God, and as the Holy Spirit assures the believer of the absolute truth and reliability of the Word of God and the gospel of Jesus Christ.

63. Believing the gospel is not a work or decision on a person's part, but rather a receiving of truth into one's heart — a receiving of Jesus Christ according to John 1:12.

64. The personal appeal to sinners to receive Christ is often made in a way contrary to Scripture by saying that God will not force a person to receive Christ, but waits for the person to open his own heart's door. On the contrary, many Scriptures clearly teach that it is only God who can open a person's heart to receive the gospel and believe. (See refs: Acts 15:9; 16:14, Rom. 10:10; 2 Cor 4:6; Gal 4:6; Heb 10:22; Rev 3:20.) Specifically, the passage in Rev 3:20 is speaking, not about one receiving Christ as Savior, but about a believer opening the door to intimate fellowship with Him.

65. The concept of "giving one's heart to Jesus" is unbiblical. Rather, the Bible says "Ye are bought with a price. . ." (I Cor 6:20;7:23) Thus, all who believe were bought by the shed blood of Christ and they wholly belong to Him by his act of sacrifice rather than by some decision on any person's part.

66. The concept of "asking Jesus to come into one's heart" is unbiblical. Any words or phrases used to convey the idea of becoming a believer in Jesus Christ which are not supported by Scripture are in danger of communicating a false gospel.

67. The "altar call", which apparently originated during the ministry of that great evangelist, Charles G. Finney, is nowhere to be found in Scripture. Although there is nothing inherently wrong or unbiblical about calling people to come to an altar to seek God, there are many abuses of the altar call in churches and by evangelists today.

68. We are commissioned as believers to witness and preach the gospel to every creature to the ends of the earth, because (1) the gospel is the power of God unto salvation to every one that believes, and (2) we do not know in advance whom God has chosen to be saved.

69. It is clearly the task of the church to carry out the Great Commission, but we must use sound biblical theology in every part of the work including calling people to repent and believe the gospel. Altar calls not based upon Scripture are outside the bounds of the Great Commission.

70. It is not the task of the church to convert people, but to make disciples of those who, by God's grace, do believe.

71. The gospel is the power of God unto salvation for every one who believes. Therefore, all who witness, minister, teach, or preach the Word must be sure to preach the Word in truth.

72. It is God's task to save and to keep those who believe. We labor with God.

73. A believer does not necessarily have to understand or know biblical doctrines in order for them to be operative in his or her life through the ministry of the Holy Spirit. However, feeding oneself on the Word of God through hearing, reading, studying, memorizing, and meditating upon the Word, and as God enables, the teaching of the Word of God to others helps the believer to understand and know God through His Word, and therefore to be able to glorify God in a greater way.

74. If a hymn or Christian song contains a single concept which is foreign to, or clearly contrary to, Scripture it should be rejected for use by the church and by all who minister in song.

75. The use of modern praise choruses during church worship services, to the exclusion of the historic and great hymns of the church is a detrimental practice because it deprives the younger generation of the rich doctrinal truths found in some of those great hymns.

76. There are many antichrists in the world. Some of them are pastors and church leaders at every level in virtually all organized denominations, fellowships, and other kinds of church organizations. "Ye shall know them by their fruits." (Matt 7:16,20)

77. The believer's will is involved in acts of good works, and service, for which he will be rewarded, but the reward is not reckoned of debt, but of grace, because it is God which works in the believer both to will and to do of His good pleasure.

78. To die, as expressed by God in Genesis 2:17, is to have one's will come in some degree under the control of Satan. When Adam chose to sin he died, and in Adam all mankind died. Therefore, even though we have physical life we are dead to God until we are born again. (2 Cor 4:4; 2 Tim 2:26; 3:13; Titus 3:3; Rev 18:23; 19:20; 20:10.)

79. The fact that the unregenerate person is dead toward God is a major proof that man is absolutely powerless to take any action of his will which would result in salvation.

80. To be given life, as expressed by Jesus Christ in John 3:16, is to have one's will, in some degree, come under the control of God. (Mk 3:35; Acts 13:36; Rom 12:2; 15:32; 1 Cor 1:1; 2 Cor 1:1; 8:5; Eph 1:1; 6:6; Col 1:1; 2 Tim 1:1; Heb 10:36; 1 Pet 4:1,2,19; 1 Jn 2:10)

81. In order to arrive at a mental and spiritual state of truly acknowledging oneself as a lost sinner in desperate need of God's salvation one must usually "come to oneself" — i.e. come to a realization that he has been dead wrong in his understanding of God, of sin, of righteousness, and of how one may get into a right relationship with God.

82. Believers must recognize and always adhere to the concept that Scripture is supreme over all formal doctrinal statements conceived by men.

83. It is evident from logic that most formal doctrinal statements held by denominations contain some error, since these doctrinal statements clash and contradict one another at various points.

84. Leaders of fellowships, denominations, and similar organizations must recognize that Scripture is supreme over all formal doctrinal statements conceived by men, and lead their people in changing such statements when God enlightens the leadership to new truth.

85. The believer's highest allegiance must be to Scripture and not to a denominational doctrinal statement.

86. As a believer in Jesus Christ when one prays for an unbeliever one must keep in mind that the unbeliever is absolutely helpless to change the course of his own spiritual life and that only God's intervention will bring about repentance unto salvation.

87. Prayer for the unbeliever should focus upon God intervening by revealing to the unbeliever his utterly lost condition and his total inability to save himself or even to move toward God.

88. A significant portion of today's evangelical church is being led astray by "prosperity gospel" preachers who are enriching themselves and fleecing the people. Prosperity in the Scriptures goes far beyond simply gaining wealth.

89. "Whatsoever a man soweth, that shall he also reap" has many applications, but the context of this passage does not support a doctrine of "give to receive" but "give from your available resources to meet the financial needs of those who have suffered financial loss." (2 Cor. 8-9) The entire passage is focused upon sharing offerings, not with a ministry, but with other believers who were in great financial need that there might be equality. (2 Cor 8:13)

90. The preaching of the gospel, when properly motivated, does not aim to convince the intellect to "make a decision for Christ" but rather to (1) help a lost person realize his lost condition, (2) to help the self-righteous person see the futility of trusting in his own works to save him, (3) to affirm the ultimate reality of heaven and hell, and (4) to point to the sacrifice of Jesus Christ on the Cross as the all-sufficient sacrifice for every sinner who comes to God.

91. To believe that a man can do anything to merit God's salvation is to rob God of His omnipotence and to make God man's debtor.

92. One of the probable reasons why such a great percentage of Charles G. Finney's converts are said to have remained faithful to God throughout their lives is that they turned to God to be saved only after reaching a clear understanding of their lost condition and that their only hope was in Jesus Christ and Him crucified. The fact that so many reached this clear understanding is evidence that the Holy Spirit was using Finney's preaching and working through it to produce the conviction of the Holy Spirit in their lives.

93. To believe that a mere man may, by his own independent decision, forfeit his salvation, is to rob God of His omnipotence. Believers are "kept by the power of God through faith." (I Pet. 1:5)

94. A Biblical view of God's sovereignty and man's inability to save himself should motivate all true believers to pray, to witness, and to teach the Bible in ways more pleasing to God, and which will more truly edify the church.

95. One major reason Jesus said, "Blessed are they that mourn . . ." (Matt 5:4a) is because it is only those who recognize and mourn the absolute lostness of man's condition who can appreciate more fully the absolute greatness of God's salvation.

The gospel is *"the power of God* unto salvation. . ."

(Romans 1:16 KJV)

The believer is "kept by *the power of God. . .*"

(1 Peter 1:5 KJV)

About the author

Leon Stansfield's Christian heritage on his father's side was Methodism. His paternal great-great grandfather was the Rev. Nathaniel Tower, a circuit-riding preacher in Indiana. Leon's mother became a believer in her thirties as the result of a lengthy spiritual journey resulting in her renewal of the salvation experience of her childhood. Leon experienced the new birth at his home a year or two later sometime during his sophomore year in high school. His family began attending an evangelical church during his junior year. He later attended Bible college for one year following high school graduation, but did not continue there after his experience there convinced him that he was not called to be a preacher, evangelist, or missionary. He was also having great difficulty gaining real assurance of salvation. He was, as are many believers who are a part of the Arminian branch of evangelicalism, woefully ignorant of the teaching of Scripture regarding assurance. He was depending upon his own works to keep him a Christian. A pivotal point in his Christian experience about six years later, was the challenge, given to him by an army buddy, Marion L. "Guy" Chiattello, in Seoul, Korea, to complete the Navigators' Topical Memory System of Bible verses during his U.S. Army service. He accepted the challenge, began the project, worked on it daily for about eighteen months, and completed the 108 verse course three months after completing army service. This and his experience of teaching Bible to Korean college students for a year during his spare time while stationed in Korea eventually led to changing his career plans from engineering to education, and later resulted in God's call to enter the Christian school ministry. He attended Bethany College, Scotts Valley, CA, received the B.S. degree in Elementary Education from Southern Oregon University, the M.Ed. degree from the University of Oregon, and completed the M.Div. degree from Christian Life School of Theology, Columbus, GA, in 2006. He is currently marketing a unique new Bible curriculum for use in grades 7-14. Read Thru The Word Bible Curriculum and other publications can be seen at www.readthrutheword.com. His wife of forty-six years, Elizabeth, is also an educator, and graduate of Southern Oregon University and the University of Oregon, having served as a teacher in most of the same locations as her husband. They have two grown children, Laura Nell, a graduate of Pepperdine University and Fuller Theological Seminary, currently teaching English in South Korea, and Craig Mark, a graduate of California State University – Fullerton, currently teaching Spanish and photography at a Christian school in southern California.

ENDNOTES:

[1] *New Catholic Encyclopedia*. Prepared by an editorial staff at the Catholic University of America, Washington, D.C. New York, McGraw-Hill, © 1967, 15 volumes, Volume 8, p. 1086.

[2] *The New Encyclopeaedia Britannica*, Macropedia, Knowledge in Depth, volume 23, University of Chicago, Fifteenth Edition, © 1985, p. 364.

[3] 1, 1086

[4] 2, 365

[5] 2, 365, bold italics by current author.

[6] 2, 365

[7] 1, 1086-7

[8] 2, 366

[9] 1, 1087

[10] MARTIN LUTHER on *THE BONDAGE OF THE WILL*, A Translation of *De Servo Arbitrio* (1525), Martin Luther's Reply To Erasmus of Rotterdam, translated by Henry Cole in 1823, public domain, The 500th Anniversary Edition (1517-2017) edited by Leon Stansfield, LEARNING LINKS PUBLISHERS, page 5.

11 Op. Cit. Page 6.

12 Op. Cit. Page 7.

13 Op. Cit. Page 9.

14 Op. Cit. Pages 9-10.

15 Op. Cit. Page 10.

16 Op. Cit. Page 11.

17 Op. Cit. Page 11.

18 Op. Cit. Pages 16-17.

19 Op. Cit. Page 17.

20 Op. Cit. Page 19.

21 Op. Cit. Pages 19-20.

22 Op. Cit. Page 20.

23 Op. Cit. Page 21.

24 Op. Cit. Pages 22-23.

25 Op. Cit. Page 23.

26 Op. Cit. Page 25.

27 Op. Cit. Pages 26-27.

28 Op. Cit. Page 28.

29 Op. Cit. Page 29.

30 Op. Cit. Pages 30-31.

31 Op. Cit. Page 31.

32 Op. Cit. Page 31.

33 Op. Cit. Page 32.

34 Op. Cit. Page 32.

35 Op. Cit. Page 32.

36 Op. Cit. Page 33.

37 Op. Cit. Pages 33-34.

38 Op. Cit. Page 34.

39 Op. Cit. Pages 34-35.

40 Op. Cit. Page 35.

41 Op. Cit. Pages 35-36.

42 Op. Cit. Page 37.

43 Op. Cit. Pages 37-38.

44 Op. Cit. Pages 38-40.

45 Op. Cit. Pages 41-43.

46 Op. Cit. Page 43.

47 Op. Cit. Page 44.

48 Op. Cit. Pages 44-45.

49 Op. Cit. Page 45.

50 Op. Cit. Page 46.

51 Op. Cit. Page 49.

52 Op. Cit. Pages 49-50.

53 Op. Cit. Page 58.

54 Op. Cit. Page 58.

55 Op. Cit. Pages 59-61

56 Op. Cit. Pages 62-68.

57 Op. Cit. Pages 70-71.

58 Op. Cit. Page 75.

59 Op. Cit. Pages 76-78.

60 Op. Cit. Pages 79-81.

61 Op. Cit. Pages 81-82.

62 Op. Cit. Pages 82-87.

63 Op. Cit. Pages 90-91.

64 Op. Cit. Pages 93-97.

65 Op. Cit. Page 97-98.

66 Op. Cit. Page 99-100.

67 Op. Cit. Page 103.

68 Op. Cit. Pages 107-108.

69 Op. Cit. Page 109.

70 Op. Cit. Pages 114-115.

71 Op. Cit. Pages 118-119.

72 Op. Cit. Page 120.

73 Op. Cit. Pages 121-123.

74 Op. Cit. Page 123.

75 Op. Cit. Pages 127-128.

76 Op. Cit. Pages 129-140.

77 Op. Cit. Pages 140-148

78 Op. Cit. Pages 148-151

79 Op. Cit. Pages 152

80 Op. Cit. Pages 153-158

81 Op. Cit. Page 159.

82 Op. Cit. Page 161.

83 Op. Cit. Page 162.

84 Op. Cit. Pages 163-164.

85 Op. Cit. Pages 165

86 Op. Cit. Pages 165-166.

87 Op. Cit. Pages 166.

88 Op. Cit. Page 167.

89 Op. Cit. Page 168.

90 Op. Cit. Page 170.

91 Op. Cit. Page 170.

92 Op. Cit. Pages 171-174.

93 Op. Cit. Pages 181-182.

94 Op. Cit. Page 186.

95 Op. Cit. Pages 186-187.

96 Op. Cit. Page 187.

97 Op. Cit. Page 188.

98 Op. Cit. Pages 189-190.

99 Op. Cit. Page 190.

100 Op. Cit. Pages 190-191.

101 Op. Cit. Pages 192-193.

102 Op. Cit. Page 194.

103 Op. Cit. Pages 201-202.

104 Op. Cit. Pages 202-203

105 Op. Cit. Page 205

106 Op. Cit. Pages 207-211.

Luther Monument in Wittenberg, Germany

www.ingramcontent.com/pod-product-compliance
Lightning Source LLC
Chambersburg PA
CBHW021053090426
42738CB00006B/317